Books of Enoch Collection

Scriptural Research Institute

Published by Digital Ink Productions, 2020.

Copyright

WHILE EVERY PRECAUTION has been taken in the preparation of this book, the publisher assumes no responsibility for errors or omissions, or for damages resulting from the use of the information contained herein.

BOOKS OF ENOCH COLLECTION

First edition. May 1, 2020.

Copyright © 2020 Scriptural Research Institute.

ISBN: 978-1-989852-24-8

The five books of Enoch were collected and translated into Greek by 200 BC, and Ge'ez by 1500 AD.

These English translations were created by the Scriptural Research Institute in 2020 from the Ge'ez translations.

The image used for the cover is 'The Fall of the Rebel Angels' by Pieter Bruegel the Elder, painted in 1562.

Contents

FORWARD..*page* 8

Book of the Watchers - Chapter 1..*page* 28

Book of the Watchers - Chapter 2..*page* 29

Book of the Watchers - Chapter 3..*page* 30

Book of the Watchers - Chapter 4..*page* 31

Book of the Watchers - Chapter 5..*page* 32

Book of the Watchers - Chapter 6..*page* 33

Book of the Watchers - Chapter 7..*page* 34

Book of the Watchers - Chapter 8..*page* 35

Book of the Watchers - Chapter 9..*page* 36

Book of the Watchers - Chapter 10..*page* 37

Book of the Watchers - Chapter 11..*page* 39

Book of the Watchers - Chapter 12..*page* 40

Book of the Watchers - Chapter 13..*page* 41

Book of the Watchers - Chapter 14..*page* 42

Book of the Watchers - Chapter 15..*page* 44

Book of the Watchers - Chapter 16..*page* 45

Book of the Watchers - Chapter 17..*page* 46

Book of the Watchers - Chapter 18..*page* 47

BOOKS OF ENOCH COLLECTION

Book of the Watchers - Chapter 19..*page* 48

Book of the Watchers - Chapter 20..*page* 49

Book of the Watchers - Chapter 21..*page* 50

Book of the Watchers - Chapter 22..*page* 51

Book of the Watchers - Chapter 23..*page* 53

Book of the Watchers - Chapter 24..*page* 54

Book of the Watchers - Chapter 25..*page* 55

Book of the Watchers - Chapter 26..*page* 56

Book of the Watchers - Chapter 27..*page* 57

Book of the Watchers - Chapter 28..*page* 58

Book of the Watchers - Chapter 29..*page* 59

Book of the Watchers - Chapter 30..*page* 60

Book of the Watchers - Chapter 31..*page* 61

Book of the Watchers - Chapter 32..*page* 62

Book of the Watchers - Chapter 33..*page* 63

Book of the Watchers - Chapter 34..*page* 64

Book of the Watchers - Chapter 35..*page* 65

Book of the Watchers - Chapter 36..*page* 66

Book of Parables - Chapter 1 (37)..*page* 67

Book of Parables - Chapter 2 (38)..*page* 68

Book of Parables - Chapter 3 (39)..*page* 69

Book of Parables - Chapter 4 (40)..*page* 71

Book of Parables - Chapter 5 (41)...*page* 72

Book of Parables - Chapter 6 (42)...*page* 74

Book of Parables - Chapter 7 (43)...*page* 75

Book of Parables - Chapter 8 (44)...*page* 76

Book of Parables - Chapter 9 (45)...*page* 77

Book of Parables - Chapter 10 (46)...*page* 78

Book of Parables - Chapter 11 (47)...*page* 79

Book of Parables - Chapter 12 (48)...*page* 80

Book of Parables - Chapter 13 (49)...*page* 81

Book of Parables - Chapter 14 (50)...*page* 82

Book of Parables - Chapter 15 (51)...*page* 83

Book of Parables - Chapter 16 (52)...*page* 84

Book of Parables - Chapter 17 (53)...*page* 85

Book of Parables - Chapter 18 (54)...*page* 86

Book of Parables - Chapter 19 (55)...*page* 87

Book of Parables - Chapter 20 (56)...*page* 88

Book of Parables - Chapter 21 (57)...*page* 89

Book of Parables - Chapter 22 (58)...*page* 90

Book of Parables - Chapter 23 (59)...*page* 91

Book of Parables - Chapter 24 (60)...*page* 92

Book of Parables - Chapter 25 (61)...*page* 95

Book of Parables - Chapter 26 (62)...*page* 97

BOOKS OF ENOCH COLLECTION

Book of Parables - Chapter 27 (63)..*page* 99

Book of Parables - Chapter 28 (64)..*page* 101

Book of Parables - Chapter 29 (65)..*page* 102

Book of Parables - Chapter 30 (66)..*page* 104

Book of Parables - Chapter 31 (67)..*page* 105

Book of Parables - Chapter 32 (68)..*page* 107

Book of Parables - Chapter 33 (69)..*page* 108

Book of Parables - Chapter 34 (70)..*page* 111

Book of Parables - Chapter 35 (71)..*page* 112

Astronomical Book - Chapter 1 (72)..*page* 114

Astronomical Book - Chapter 2 (73)..*page* 117

Astronomical Book - Chapter 3 (74)..*page* 118

Astronomical Book - Chapter 4 (75)..*page* 120

Astronomical Book - Chapter 5 (76)..*page* 121

Astronomical Book - Chapter 6 (77)..*page* 123

Astronomical Book - Chapter 7 (78)..*page* 124

Astronomical Book - Chapter 8 (79)..*page* 126

Astronomical Book - Chapter 9 (80)..*page* 127

Astronomical Book - Chapter 10 (81)..*page* 128

Astronomical Book - Chapter 11 (82)..*page* 129

Dream Visions - Chapter 1 (83)..*page* 131

Dream Visions - Chapter 2 (84)..*page* 133

Dream Visions - Chapter 3 (85)..*page* 134

Dream Visions - Chapter 4 (86)..*page* 135

Dream Visions - Chapter 5 (87)..*page* 136

Dream Visions - Chapter 6 (88)..*page* 137

Dream Visions - Chapter 7 (89)..*page* 138

Dream Visions - Chapter 7 Interpreted......................................*page* 144

Dream Visions - Chapter 8 (90)..*page* 151

Dream Visions - Chapter 8 Interpreted......................................*page* 155

Letter of Enoch - Chapter 1 (91)..*page* 159

Letter of Enoch - Chapter 2 (92)..*page* 161

Letter of Enoch - Chapter 3 (93)..*page* 162

Letter of Enoch - Chapter 4 (94)..*page* 164

Letter of Enoch - Chapter 5 (95)..*page* 165

Letter of Enoch - Chapter 6 (96)..*page* 166

Letter of Enoch - Chapter 7 (97)..*page* 167

Letter of Enoch - Chapter 8 (98)..*page* 168

Letter of Enoch - Chapter 9 (99)..*page* 170

Letter of Enoch - Chapter 10 (100)..*page* 172

Letter of Enoch - Chapter 11 (101)..*page* 174

Letter of Enoch - Chapter 12 (102)..*page* 175

Letter of Enoch - Chapter 13 (103)..*page* 176

Letter of Enoch - Chapter 14 (104)..*page* 178

BOOKS OF ENOCH COLLECTION

Letter of Enoch - Chapter 15 (105)..*page* 180

Letter of Enoch - Chapter 16 (106)..*page* 181

Letter of Enoch - Chapter 17 (107)..*page* 183

Letter of Enoch - Chapter 18 (108)..*page* 184

Book of the Watchers Notes..*page* 186

Book of Parables Notes...*page* 194

Astronomical Book Notes...*page* 207

Dream Visions Notes...*page* 212

Letter of Enoch Notes..*page* 215

Forward

THE FIVE BOOKS OF ENOCH are a collection of books written in Semitic languages, and often grouped together as the 'Book of Enoch,' or '1st Enoch.' The books were likely written at different points in time and different Semitic languages. The first book was the Book of the Watchers, which is generally considered to be the oldest book in the collection, however, the age of the book is debated. The book is now known to have originated long before Christianity since the discovery of the Dead Sea Scrolls, however, was lost for well over a thousand years to Europeans, and assumed to be a Christian-era work when the Europeans rediscovered it in Ethiopia. The five books of Enoch only survive in Ge'ez, the classical language of Ethiopia, however, do not survive intact, and some sections of text do not survive.

The Ge'ez texts are believed to be translations from a Greek source, which was itself a translation of an Aramaic source. Many fragments of the Aramaic texts were discovered among the Dead Sea scrolls, as well as Hebrew and Greek fragments. The Aramaic texts are mostly the same as the Ge'ez texts, however, scroll 4Q209 also includes a section of text from 3rd Book of Enoch, the Astronomical Book, which is lost from the Ge'ez copies. A few fragments of Greek translations have been found in Egypt in the past two centuries, which generally match the Ge'ez translation. A small fragment of a Latin translation was also preserved by the Vatican through the centuries, which also matches the Ge'ez copies for a small fragment of 4th Book of Enoch, Dream Visions.

Other books attributed to Enoch, including the Secrets of Enoch, which is also called the 2nd Book of Enoch, however, is not the same text as the Semitic 2nd Book of Enoch. The Secrets of Enoch has only survived in the Old Slavonic language in the Balkan Peninsula and may be a partial paraphrase of the Book of the Watchers. Another text attributed to Enoch is the Revelation of Metatron, also called the Revelation of Metatron, Book of the Palaces, Book of Rabbi Ishmael the High Priest, or the 3rd Book of Enoch, however, is not the same text as the Semitic 3rd Book of Enoch, or any section of the Semitic books of

Enoch. The Revelation of Metatron is written as a sequel to the first five books of Enoch and is written from the perspective of Enoch in the sky, where his angelic name was Metatron. The Revelation of Metatron appears to have been written in Hebrew but includes several Greek and Latin words that have led scholars to assume the text is a Jewish text written in the Christian era.

Most of the iconography in the Book of the Watchers points to a Canaanite origin, as does the astronomical references to the seven stars beyond the eastern edge of the world, which was the situation between 2300 and 2000 BC when the Pleiades star cluster was the morning stars. The Pleiades star cluster is a group of stars in the constellation of Taurus. They are easily seen in the northern hemisphere, as well as at equatorial latitudes, and have historically been widely used to navigate by. The Greek name is believed to derive from the word meaning 'sail' (πλέω). The name Pleiades appears in both the Septuagint and Masoretic Texts, which is one of the few times the two documents agree on the names of the stars. This indicates the name may not have been redacted in this case, however, it was likely the original term would have been Aziz, the morning star, as this star or group of stars is listed in contrast to the evening star. Throughout all of ancient history, the merchant season in the Mediterranean began with the helical rising of the Pleiades, which shows the importance of the star cluster to the Canaanites, and their ancient trading partners. The Pleiades were rising in the vernal equinox around 2300 BC, which means they would have been seen as the 'morning stars' of their time. By 2000 BC the Pleiades would have no longer been the morning stars but did continue to be used for navigation throughout recorded history.

All of the five Ge'ez Books of Enoch and the Revelation of Metatron use the term watcher, which was replaced by grigori in the Secrets of Enoch. The word grigori is believed to have been the Old Slavonic transliteration of the Greek word egrêgoroe (ἐγρήγοροι), meaning 'watchful.' The term watcher is often mistranslated as 'angel' in modern translation, however, the term angel is not in the five books of Enoch. The term angel does show up in both the Secrets of Enoch and the Revelation of Metatron, however, as both texts were translated into Greek, the term could have been inserted at that time. Some of the watchers mentioned by name do have the same names as angels in other Hebrew scriptures, as well as later Christian and Islamic texts. This implies that the watchers are angels, yet the word was not used, which points to an earlier language that did not use the word angels like Hebrew did, such as Canaanite.

The watchers as believed to be based on an older Sumerian and Akkadian story of the igigi. The igigi were a group of beings in the ancient Akkadian creation and flood mythology who played a similar role to the watchers in the Enochian literature. The Aramaic term 'watchers' was iri (עִיר), which the Akkadian word igigi was composed of the Akkadian words 'igi' and 'gi' meaning 'eyes' and 'penetrate sexually.' The similar nature of 'eyes' (igi) and 'watchers' (iri) is difficult to ignore, however, the 'sexual violation' of humans is what the watchers were accused of in the books of Enoch. The Book of Parables contains several terms that appear to be direct translations of Akkadian terms from the Akkadian creation and flood stories, which supports the idea that the watchers began as a Canaanite version of the igigi.

The existing text of the Book of the Watchers appears to have been pieced together, at some point before the Dead Sea scrolls were collected, as they generally match the surviving Ge'ez translations, as well as surviving Hebrew, Greek, and Latin fragments proving the text was fairly standardized by 300 BC. The surviving copies all have repeating stories, such as the description of the seven stars beyond the eastern edge of the world, which took place in both chapters 18 and 21. These repeating stories point to the text being compiled from older texts into an Aramaic or Hebrew text, much like some of the texts of the Torah.

The Book of Parables is unique in that no fragments of it have yet been documented within the Dead Sea scrolls. As the Books of Enoch have traditionally been used by the Beta-Israel community, and it is likely a book they carried south from Egypt to Kush and later the Ethiopian highlands, the Book of Parables must have been part of the collection before 200 BC, as their primary holy book, the Orit, is based on an early Greek version of the Septuagint in circulation between circa 225 and 200 BC, which only had eight books. After 200 BC, additional books had been translated by the Library of Alexandria, and therefore, if they left Egypt after 200 BC, they would have had a larger collection of holy-books.

The origin of the Book of Parables is widely debated, with scholars generally ignoring the history of the text within the Beta-Israel community, and instead claiming it was a Christian-era book, written anywhere between 50 and 270 AD. There are several reasons why it is assumed to be a Christian era text, even though it is clearly not a Christian text, but these 'pieces of evidence' have all been manufactured by the translators, who assumed it was a Christian era text, and interpreted the text using Christian terminology. The most obvious example it the phrase 'son of man' generally used throughout the Book of Parables, which is seen as a reference to Jesus Christ. Simply reading the text proves the text has nothing to do with Jesus Christ, and although it could be read as a prophetic text, was prophesying the flood of Noah, not the coming of the messiah, like most Messianic Jewish works. The person being referenced in the Book of Parables as the 'son of man' is quite obviously Seth, the patriarch of all the humans that survived the flood. The Hebrew ben-'adam (בן–אדם) which is translated as 'son of man' is also 'son of Adam,' which Seth it introduced as in the open lines. The only way to translate the meaningless term 'son of man' is to impose a Christian framework on the book, forcing it to in the end 'look Christian' even if there is nothing Christian about it.

The Book of Parables if divided largely into three parables that are obviously not from the same era. The second parable is a paraphrasing of the ancient Babylonian flood narratives, and some specifically Babylonian elements remain in the text, such as the references to Abzu and Tiamat in chapter 18. In the Mesopotamian creation mythology, inherited from the earlier Sumerian and Akkadian creation mythology Abzu was a god that represented the freshwater ocean above the sky, while Tiamat the goddess that represented was the saltwater ocean beneath the world. The two once united to flood the earth, killing everyone except Ziusudra and the people and animals in his houseboat. The reference to these two Mesopotamian gods within the Second Parable proves this parable originated during the Neo-Babylonian era, or earlier, as the Hebrews were not influenced by Babylonian mythology later under the Persians, Greeks, or Romans.

Both of the first two parables contain Babylonian elements, including the term 'Lord of Spirit,' which continues through the third parable, but it not found in other Jewish texts. The term is a direct translation of Ellil, the name of the Akkadian god that caused the flood in the Mesopotamian flood mythology. By the Neo-Babylonian Empire, Ellil was no longer being worshiped by the Babylonians, having first having to have been replaced by Marduk during the Old Babylonian era, and then Bel in the Neo-Babylonian era, who was mentioned in the Septuagint's translation of the Book of Daniel which was set in the Neo-Babylonian Empire. Several copies of the Mesopotamian flood story have survived of the present, including the Instructions of Shuruppak dated to circa 2600 BC, the Epic of Gilgamesh dated to circa 1800 BC, the Epic of Atra-Hasis dated to circa 1650 BC, and the Eridu Genesis dated to circa 1600 BC. In all of these copies, the god that caused the flood was Ellil whose name translates as 'Lord of Wind,' 'Lord of Breath,' or 'Lord of Spirit.'

The Noah character in the Mesopotamian flood epics had several names depending on the era, including Ziusudra, Utnapishtim, and Atra-Hasis. The name Ziusudra was the term used in the Persian era and was translated into Greek as Xisuthros (Ξίσουθρος). Ziusudra translates as "life of long days," which could be the source of the strange title 'Head of Days,' found in the Book of Paraphrases. The term 'Head of Days' is often assumed to be a mistranslation of the term 'Ancient of Days,' which is also found in the Book of Daniel, however, the Book of Daniel is considered to be a later work written in the 2nd-century-BC, meaning the term 'Ancient of Days' is more likely a corruption of 'Head of Days.' In the closing chapter of the Book of Parables, the Head of Days is referred to as 'that Head of Days,' implying this was a title, and there was more than one. This appears to parallel the Noah character in the Hindu religion, Manu, whose name means 'man' or 'human' like Adam. In the Sanskrit text the Manusmriti, Manu was the survivor of a flood along with other people he saved in his boat. The term Manu is used as a title, as he is the father of the new race of humans after the flood, and it is a title many Manus have held in the cycles of destruction and rebuilding according to the Manusmriti. This text is considered to be a composite of ancient texts standards into its current version during the Greek-era, circa 200 BC. The archaic language found in some sections of the Manusmriti has led some linguists to claim that the older sections could not date to between 1250 and 1000 BC, and the text is believed to have circulated within the Persian empire, like the other Sanskrit texts of the time.

The second parable, while using the same reference to the ancient god Enlil and a title that seems derived from the title of Ziusudra, dates itself to the beginning of the Persian era, between 539 BC and 525 BC, when it refers to the invading Medes and Persian in chapter 20. The Medes and Persians were two Iranian peoples in modern Iran, who conquered two significant empires in the Middle East between the 8th and 4th centuries BC and play a significant role in the ancient Hebrew texts. The Medes rebelled from the Assyrian Empire in 616 BC, and ultimately conquered most of it by 609 BC, including the territory of the Persians to the south of Media. The Persians then revolted from the Medes in 553 BC, and conquered the Medes in 550 BC, followed by their allies the Neo-Babylonian Empire in 539 BC. The Neo-Babylonians had already conquered the Judeans, and so Judea became a Persian territory, in theory, however, the Persian army did not occupy the region until around 525 BC when King Cambyses occupied Phoenicia, which was followed by an invasion of Egypt the following year. Between 539 and 525 BC, Judea was essentially independent, although according to the Hebrew books of the scribe Ezra, Judea never rebelled against the Persians. These books of Ezra tell the stories of Ezra and Nehemiah, who were both apparently were sent by the King of Persia to rebuild the Temple in Jerusalem, and restore the eternal-fire using naphtha, meaning, they were both there to build a Zoroastrian fire-temple in Jerusalem. Some Jewish texts do describe the Persians, Medes, and Chaldeans (Babylonians), as corruptors of the temple, which is clearly the view of the priesthoods that Ezra evicted from the temple they were already rebuilding when he arrived.

In chapter 20 of the Book of Parables, as the Medes and Persians are invading, the author predicts at Jerusalem will stand before them, meaning this is before the occupation in 525 BC. The only time the Medes and Persians ever invaded Judea was in 525 BC. The Parthians did invade Judea in 40 BC, and set up the puppet state of King Antigonus II Mattathias, the last Jewish king of the Hasmonean dynasty, however, by that time the Medes no longer a significant people in Persian. In 129 BC the Medes had revolted against the Greek rule of the Parthian Empire and had been brutally suppressed. They never recovered as a people and were absorbed into the Persian population. If this story in the Book of Parables was set during the Parthian invasion, Greeks and Persians would have been mentioned, not Medes and Persians. The next invasion of the Levant by the Persians was during the Byzantine-Sassanian war of 602 to 628, when the Persians, no longer under Greek influence did occupy Judea, however, there still would have been no reason to mention the Medes, a people that had effectively ceased to exist 700 years earlier. The only time this reference to the invading Medes and Persians can be dated to was between 539 and 525 BC, meaning the second parable had to date to that time.

One chapter of the third parable is clearly much later though, written under significant Zoroastrian influence. Zoroastrianism was the ancient religion of the Persian peoples, which was later brutally suppressed by Alexander the Great. In chapter 22, the Zoroastrian end-of-the-world is described, which is entirely different from the Jewish and Christian ends-of-the-world. In the Zoroastrian world view, everything was part of the overarching battle between light and darkness. All good things including light, heat, fire, wisdom, knowledge, and even God in some sects of the religion, were seen as part of the light, while everything negative was seen as part of the darkness. The end of the world in Zoroastrianism was predicted to come when the light finally conquered darkness, which is described in chapter 22. This chapter of the third parable could only have been written during the Persian era, as Hellenic Judaism was closer to Rabbinic Judaism and Christianity than Zoroastrianism. No known sect of Jews or Christians ever held views similar to the Zoroastrians on the issue of how the world will end, and therefore this cannot be dated to a later period.

The third parable also included the first reference to Lord Moloch in the books of Enoch, which continues through the later books. The references begin in chapter 27 and are anachronistic in a Persian era document, as Lord Moloch appears to had disappeared from Israelite and Jewish texts after the book of Amos, which should have been written sometime circa 750 BC. According to the Hebrew scriptures, the prophet Amos preached in Samaria between 760 and 755 BC during the rule of King Jeroboam II, and criticized the Samaritans for worshiping Moloch. Amos also mentioned that there was a star or stars associated with Moloch, implying that the books of Enoch could have been the holy texts used by the Samaritans at the time, as clearly the Torah was not since it prohibited worshiping Moloch. At the time the Samaritans controlled a kingdom north of Judea in the territory of northern Israel, northern Palestinian West

Bank, southern Israel, and southern Syria. This is the same territory that the books of Enoch are set in. If the books of Enoch are the remnants of of the Samaritan holy books from before they were conquered by the Assyrians, then they would have been in use by 755 BC, likely in a book from Noah's perspective and another from Methuselah's perspective.

Lord Moloch is known from a few ancient Canaanite texts and was the national god of Ammon (modern Amman, the capital of Jordan) when the Torah's book of Levites was written. He is known from ancient Hebrew texts as v'l mlch (מלך בעל), also transliterated as Ba'al Moloch or Lord Moloch, however, there are several variations, including Molech, Mollok, Milcom, or Malcam. The Greek transliteration in the Septuagint was Molokh (Μολοχ), and the Latin translation in the Vulgate was Moloch, which is where the English transliteration originated.

Moloch is poorly understood Canaanite god, which appears to be earliest of the first Canaanite gods that Israelites were banned from worshiping, specifically prohibited by Moses in the Torah. The god seems to have quickly been abandoned and little evidence remains of him in the archaeological records. There is a reference to a god named MLK in the Ugaritic Texts from between 1450 and 1200 BC, which is believed to be Moloch, but little is known about that god. Based on the description of Moloch in the 4th Book of Enoch, Dream Visions, he appears to have been the sun. The idea that he was a solar god has been proposed by scholars for centuries, however, so far there is no archaeological evidence either supporting or contradicting this conclusion.

The name Moloch (מֹלֶךְ) is derived from the same root term MLK as melech (מֶלֶךְ) meaning 'king,' and spelled the same way in ancient Hebrew, however pronounced differently. It is theorized that the name of the god was the Canaanite word 'King,' which implies that if 'Lord Moloch' replaced another name in the texts as 'Lord of Spirit' appears to have replaced 'Ellil,' it was likely also Ellil, as Ellil's title was the 'King of the Gods.' The Syrians did later have a god known as Malakbel during the Greek era, however, this translates as 'Angel/Messenger of the Lord/Bel' not 'Moloch the Lord.' Malakbel could be a later development from Ba'al Moloch, which support the northern Canaanite origin, and not a southern origin were the Hebrews settled. The mention of MLK in the Ugaritic Texts also supports the northern origin, as Ugarit was one of the most northern cities also the coast of Canaan, laying on the northern coast of Syria today.

The Astronomical Book explains a very different version of reality from the one that most people believe in today: a flat world with a physical sky above it. In this other world, the sun, moon, and stars all enter the space under the sky through portals at the east edge of the world and exit through the portals at the western edge of the world. The Astronomical Book attempts to explain the movement of the sun, moon, and winds, and is sometimes referred to as the Enochian Calendar, as it tried to explain the way the days, months, and years pass over time, and how the winds changed through the year. The world described is similar to the ancient Babylonian world view, which many ancient cultures inherited and used until the Greek philosopher Eratosthenes proposed the alternate concept that the world was spherical around 240 BC. The two world-systems were debated until the Imperial Church of Rome officially endorsed the flat Earth, which became the standard European world-view until the time of Copernicus.

The Astronomical Book does not have many unique terms or descriptions of events to date it by like the other books of Enoch. There are many unique names found in the Astronomical Book but most cannot be traced back to a specific language or culture, and are therefore not useful for dating the text. The surviving fragments found among the Dead Sea scrolls are accepted as dating back to the 3rd-century BC, however, the book could be significantly older. The names of the sun in chapter 7 could indicate that some of the text originated in the Old Kingdom of Egypt. The names are listed as Orjares and Tomas are possibly based on the Egyptian terms Her-ur and Atum, which were pronounced as *her-wer* and *tmw* respectively, and were both solar gods. If both terms were translated into Greek by translators that did not recognize the original names, they would become approximately *Erweros* and *Tomwos*, which could them have become the present forms when translated into Ge'ez. Her-ur was the national god in the first few dynasties of the Old Kingdom, however, he had been replaced by the sun-god Ra by the 5th Dynasty. By the Middle Kingdom, Her-ur was replaced by Osiris as the husband of Isis and the father of Horus the younger. If the name Orjares is a corruption of Her-ur, the date of the original text would most-likely date back to before the 5th-Dynasty, and almost certainly before the Middle Kingdom. On the other hand, Atum continued to be worshiped until the New Kingdom, and based on the Letter of Aristeas and the Pithom Stele, was believed to have been Moses' original god by some Jews and Greeks at the time the Septuagint was translated at the Library of Alexandria.

The name Milki-El also shows up in the Astronomical Book, as a name of a star, and is otherwise known as the name of a Canaanite official in the Amarna Period when Akhenaten was instituting his one-god policy in Egypt, around 1340 BC. While it is unknown if the official was named after a star, but it does prove the name itself was Canaanite, which points to a Canaanite origin for the list of star names. While there are many Canaanite names and terms in ancient Hebrew texts, most of these terms appear in the earliest texts such as the Torah and book of Job, which indicates the Astronomical Book is also an early text. The fact that Enoch is mentioned in the Torah and is unique within the Torah as someone who was taken to heaven and brought back to the Earth, yet his entire story is told in less that one chapter of the book of Genesis, implies that some of the Books of Enoch were in circulation when the book of Genesis was written.

The book of Dream Visions, also called the Animal Apocalypse, appears to been compiled from an older Canaanite text in the early Persian era and was likely attached to the Astronomical Book from the beginning. The Astronomical Book was written from the view of Methuselah, Enoch's son, which Dream Visions continues, however, the majority of the text could not date to before the early Persian era. The book of Dreams and Visions is likely the first attempt to retell the history of the world from the point of view of sheep. In this case Israeli sheep, who had to contend with Egyptian wolves, Philistine dogs, Babylonian lions, and Persian eagles. The first six chapters of the book seem like it was attached to the Astronomical Book, along with the beginning of chapter 7, which includes the vision of the sky collapsing and the earth being flooded. This vision of Noah's flood matches the description of the world found in the Astronomical Book, which includes a solid sky above the world, with water above it.

After Noah and his three bull sons survived the flood, the species switched from bulls to sheep, indicating the likely point where the original text was extended. These sheep then live out the general history of the Israelites found in the Torah, and some other early Hebrew texts found in the Tanakh (Old Testament). There are a few points where the book of Dream Visions deviates from the other Hebrew texts, such as claiming that the Israelites were descendants of Japheth instead of Shem. Chapters 7 and 8 are both very long in comparison to the first six chapters, supporting the idea that they were an extension to the original work, however, they end with the Persian eagles being destroyed by a God, referred to as the Lord of Sheep, coming down from the sky and slaughtering the Persians and their allies, and then rebuilding a better temple than the temple that was being worshiped at. The author's view of the temple and the priests that were sent out from it show that he (or she) was not associated with the temple, and viewed the priests as corrupt, a common sentiment expressed in Second Temple era texts.

The description of Solomon's Temple, as well as the Second Temple, is unusual as is described the temple as having a high watchtower, which was not in the description of Solomon's Temple in other ancient texts. As the author could not have seen Solomon's Temple, it is likely that this is a description of the Second Temple and would explain the tower mentioned in the description of the Second Temple in the Letter of Aristeas. The high high-tower is reminiscent of the 'high watch post' (Hara Berezaiti) in the Zoroastrian religion, which was supposed to be high above the world on a sacred mountain at the north pole. The ruins of many ancient Zoroastrian fire temples throughout the lands of the old Persian Empire include towers, supporting the idea that Ezra and Nehemiah built a Zoroastrian fire-temple in Jerusalem. Unfortunately, as the Romans destroyed the Temple after the Second Jewish-Roman war there is no way to examine the temple's ruins today to confirm it was a fire-temple, however, both Ezra and Nehemiah stoke about 'restoring' the eternal fire in the temple, and Nehemiah even went so far as to mention naphtha, which was the petroleum fuel the Zoroastrians used to kept their sacred fires burning. As the Torah does not mention the fire in the tabernacle or the temple being eternal, this must have been an attempt to Zoroastrianize Judaism.

The book of Dream Visions also deviates from the general Messianic-Judaism concepts of the time, by having the Lord of sheep himself come down to the

Earth to rescue the Israeli sheep. This was not a supernatural Messianic warrior, like in the Jewish Apocalypse of Ezra, or the return of Elijah as some texts predicted, it was clearly a prediction that God would come down from the sky. The Lord of sheep was also predicted to thrown the fallen stars that mislead humanity into a fiery abyss, along with the shepherd priests who misled the Israeli sheep, indicating how much the author despised the priesthoods at the time. This points to someone well outside the mainstream Jewish or Samaritan population, possibly from one of the Jewish priests that Ezra had evicted from the temple when he arrived from Babylon. Given the confusing nature of the animal metaphors, especially in chapters 7 and 8, both of these chapters are included in both as non-interpreted translation and an interpreted version which explains the animals if it is clear who they represented. Many of the animals are obvious based on their actions within the story, such as the Egyptian wolves who did not want to let the Israelite sheep leave Egypt, and the Philistine dogs who fought King Saul. The identification of the Babylonian lions and Persian eagles are both based on the fact that they were the national animals of those Empires. Many other animals are also mentioned in supporting roles, however, it is not clear from context who they represented, such as the vultures and kites that accompanied the Persian eagles. Likely either the vultures or the kites were the Medes, however, it is not clear which from the context, and therefore they are left uninterpreted.

The Letter of Enoch is the fifth and final book of the five books that have survived in the Ge'ez language. Fragments of it have been found among the Dead Sea Scrolls, along with fragments of the Book of the Watchers, Book of Parables, and Dream Visions, proving it has circulated with them since at least the 3rd-century BC. It is very unlikely that the Letter of Enoch predates the 3rd-century BC, as it includes Greek philosophical ideas that unlikely to have been adopted before Alexander conquered the Persian Empire, and Greeks began ruling Judea. One of these ideas is the concept of the 'Word,' the 'first-born of God' who was accepted by Hellenistic Jews as being the 'Angel of the Lord' from the Septuagint translation of the Hebrew scriptures. Philo of Alexandria wrote about the Word (λόγος) and described it similarly to the later Christian interpretation found in the Gospel of John. Philo's writing is dated the early-1st-century AD, while the Gospel of John did not appear until the late-1st or early-2nd-century AD.

The term 'Word' in this context was developed in the Greek philosophy as the concept of the Logos (λόγος) which was based on the common Greek expression 'lego' (λέγω) meaning 'I say.' The concept entered into Jewish though sometime during the Greek era and then entered into Gnosticism in the 1st century AD, and Christianity in the 2nd-century AD. The term is first known to have been used by the Greek philosopher Heraclitus around 500 BC, who used the term to define a type of absolute knowledge. It was subsequently built on by Plato, Aristotle, the Sophists, Pyrrhonists, and Stoics by 300 BC. It is unclear when the concept entered into Judaism, however, it is clear it had entered Judaism before Gnosticism or Christianity. Philo used the term Logos similar to the later Gnostics and Christians, when he referred to the Logos of God as being the 'Angel of the Lord' from the Septuagint, and described the Word as the 'first-born of God.' This is very similar to the Christian interpretation of the Word found in the Gospel of John, except that Jesus is identified as being the Word in the Christian version.

The fact that the Word is mentioned in the Letter of Enoch does cause some confusion as it stopped being used in Judaism after the Second Jewish-Roman War, and most assume it is a Christian reference. If it is the Christian term being used, it would have to be a later addition to the text, as fragments of the Letter have been found among the Dead Sea Scrolls dating to sometime between 300 and 200 BC, however, there is no reason to assume it is the Christian term, as the Jews had a similar term. Unfortunately, the verse in question has not been recovered among the dead sea scrolls, and therefore there is no way of knowing if the term was in the original Letter or added by a Christian later on. If it was in the original text, it would date the text firmly to sometime after the Greeks had taken control of Judea, and before the Maccabean Revolt, between 330 and 167 BC.

The general message of the Letter is very Zoroastrian in its message of good-versus-bad, light-versus-dark, and righteous-versus-dishonest. The author was clearly an outcast from the power-structure of the time, and constantly attacks against the 'wealthy' and 'powerful,' accusing them of being sinful. Whoever the author was, there are very few of the indicators from the Book of the Watchers and the Book of Parables which point to Canaanite and Babylonian origins for the text, and the little present can be explained as copying from the earlier texts. The identical description of the sky becoming seven times brighter when the end of the world comes is identical to the description found in the Book of Parables, which is otherwise anachronistic in the Book of Parables, as all other indicators point to a Jewish reworking of a Babylonian text, likely during the Babylonian era. This idea that the world would end in light when good/light conquered evil/darkness, is the central theme of Zoroastrianism, the official religion of the Persian Empire that ruled Judea between 525 and 333 BC. The identical description of the end of the world in the Book of Parables and the Letter of Enoch, suggests strongly that the author of the Letter was the same person that added the description of the end-of-the-world to the Book of Parables, likely at the same time that the 'Testament of Noah' was redacted into the surviving Book of Parables.

The major subject of the Letter of Enoch, which has caused a great deal of debate for millennia, is the question of which calendar the author was using when he made his predictions. In the Letter Enoch divides the history of the world into 10 'weeks,' with Adam being made at the beginning of the first 'week,' and the end of the world coming at the end of the tenth 'week.' This way of telling time is virtually unique to the Letter, however, the author was presumably using some calendar that he expected others to understand. The idea that the author was using 'weeks' has often led to the Letter being associated with the Book of Jubilees, which likewise uses a system of 'weeks' to describe periods longer than a year, however, the 'weeks' in Jubilees are seven years long, which makes the association with the Jubilees calendar irrelevant, as the world would have ended 70 years after God made Adam.

To understand the 'weeks' the author was intending, either the concept of a fixed 'week' of time needs to be dismissed, and the length of time is variable, or a logical assumption needs to be made that the end of the world at the end of the 10th 'week' is related to the end-of-the-world prediction in the Book of the Watchers, which dates it to 10,000 years after the time of Enoch. As it's unclear which version of the Torah the author of the Letter would have had, it is unclear which chronology he was using, however, the chronology of the Septuagint appears closest to the predictions in the Letter of Enoch. Given the similarity between the 10,000-year prediction of the end of the world after the time of Enoch in the Book of the Watchers, and the 12,000-year cycle of creation and destruction in the Zoroastrian religion, it seems likely that the calendar would have been based on 10 'weeks' of 1200 years. This is similar to the Mesopotamian 'ners' of 600 years, and 'sars' of 3600 years.

It's unclear which chronology the author would have used, as, in the Masoretic text Enoch lived between 622 and 987 AM (MT), while in the Greek Septuagint Enoch lived between 1122 and 1487 AM (GS), and in the Samaritan Torah Enoch lived between 522 and 887 AM (ST). As a result of the differences in the texts, there are different versions of the Anno Mundi calendar, which based on the number of years since Adam was created in the various Israelite religions. Given the differences in the texts, the Enochian prediction of the end of the world can only be placed into the broad time-span of sometime between 10,500 and 11,500 AM. By the Persian era, this time-span would have looked like the Zoroastrian 12,000-year cycle. Given the descriptions of the end-of-the-world in the Book of Parables, chapter 22, repeated in this book in chapter 1, it is clear there was a Zoroastrian influence in these texts. If the ten 'weeks' are 1200 years long each, then the length of the 10 'weeks' would have been 12,000 years, and Enoch would have been born in the first 'week' regardless of the texts used. Using this timescale the 10 weeks of destruction are, using the Anno Mundi (AM) calendar for comparison:

Week 1: 1 to 1200 AM (statement: Enoch was born near end)

- Septuagint chronology: 5534 to 4335 BC (Enoch's birth: 1122 AM / 4412 BC)

- Masoretic chronology: 3774 to 2575 BC (Enoch's birth: 622 AM / 3152 BC)

- Samaritan chronology: 4415 to 3216 BC (Enoch's birth: 522 AM / 3893 BC)

Week 2: 1201 to 2400 AM (prediction: Noah survives flood)

- Septuagint chronology: 4334 to 3135 BC (Noah's flood: 2236 AM / 3298 BC)

- Masoretic chronology: 2574 to 1375 BC (Noah's flood: 1656 AM / 2118 BC)

- Samaritan chronology: 3215 to 2016 BC (Noah's flood: 1307 AM / 3108 BC)

Week 3: 2401 to 3600 AM (prediction: Seed of Righteous born at the end)

- Septuagint chronology: 3134 to 1935 BC (Levi born: 3595 AM / 1939 BC)

- Masoretic chronology: 1374 to 175 BC (Maccabean Revolt began: 3599 AM / 167 BC)

- Samaritan chronology: 2015 to 816 BC (Nothing significant recorded in Samaritan Chronicle)

Week 4: 3601 to 4800 AM (prediction: Visions of holy of righteous will be seen)

- Septuagint chronology: 1934 to 735 BC (Time when the Torah was written)

- Masoretic chronology: 174 BC to 1025 AD (after the predictions would have been written)

- Samaritan chronology: 815 to 384 BC (Nothing significant recorded in Samaritan Chronicle)

Week 5: 4801 to 6000 AM (prediction: house of glory and dominion will be built forever)

- Septuagint chronology: 734 BC to 465 AD (Second Temple was built)

- Masoretic chronology: 1026 to 2225 AD (after the predictions would have been written)

- Samaritan chronology: 385 to 1584 AD (after the predictions would have been written)

Week 6: 6001 to 7200 AM (prediction: race of the chosen root will be dispersed)

- Septuagint chronology: 466 to 1665 AD

- Masoretic chronology: 2226 to 3425 AD

- Samaritan chronology: 1585 to 2784 AD

Week 7: 7201 to 8400 AM (prediction: apostate generation will rise)

- Septuagint chronology: 1666 to 2865 AD

- Masoretic chronology: 3426 to 4625 AD

- Samaritan chronology: 2785 to 3984 AD

Week 8: 8401 to 9600 AM (prediction: a sword will be given to the righteous)

- Septuagint chronology: 2866 to 4065 AD

- Masoretic chronology: 4626 to 5825 AD

- Samaritan chronology: 3985 to 5184 AD

Week 9: 9601 to 10,800 AM (prediction: righteous judgment will be revealed to the whole world)

- Septuagint chronology: 4066 to 5265 AD

- Masoretic chronology: 5826 to 7025 AD

- Samaritan chronology: 5185 to 6384 AD

Week 10: 10,801 to 12,000 AM (prediction: end of the world)

- Septuagint chronology: 5266 to 6465 AD

- Masoretic chronology: 7026 to 8225 AD

- Samaritan chronology: 6385 to 7584 AD

Obviously, the easiest way to deal with the question of the weeks is to simply interpret them as 'lengths of time' that do not actually correspond to a known length of time; philosophical weeks. If the weeks are taken literally then they seem to predict things that will not happen for thousands of years. Certainly, the end-of-the-world hasn't happened yet, however, why the author would write this text is confusing. He constantly attacks those with wealth or power, predicting that they will die suddenly, but then extols his readers to follow the path of peace, and reject violence. To some degree the text seems almost early-Buddhist, attacking the wealthy while praising the poor, and rejecting violence. Certainly, there were Buddhists in the eastern regions of the Persian Empire, although their presence in the west, and influence on Judaism and later Christianity has been a matter of great debate.

The books of Enoch were not used by the Pharisees or Sadducees, yet the text did exist in Hebrew, which implies the texts may have been used by an earlier sect of Jews or Israelites. Some of the references in the Book of the Watchers do point to a Zoroastrian influence, which is generally accepted as pointing to a Persian era origin for the book, however, could also point to the date of the translation of the current version of the book into Hebrew, which could not have happened before the Persian era. Another possibility is that the Zoroastrian influence could have entered the text during the Canaanite at an earlier period, as Indo-Iranians were also present in the Mitanni Empire in the territory of Syria circa 1500 to 1300 BC, as well as in the Habiru marauders between 1800 and 1200 BC. The Hebrew fragments of the books of Enoch that have survived, are from both the Book of the Watchers and the Letter of Enoch, meaning both of the first and fifth books likely date to the Persian-era. The Aramaic fragments recovered among the Dead Sea scrolls include sections of all five texts other than the second book, the Book of Parables, which only survives in the Ge'ez language, meaning all sections other than the second book must have existed by 150 BC, and likely before 330 BC.

None of the books of Enoch appear to have been used by any known Jewish sect, although they are often theorized to have been used by the Essenes, a large but poorly documented group of non-politically active Jews during the Second Temple era. The idea that Enoch was used by the Essenes is largely based on the early assumption that the Dead Sea scrolls were a cache of their writings, however, this idea was overturned when it was realized that the scrolls represented hundreds of years worth of texts, deposited over the centuries, and represented several competing views of Judaism. Moreover, based on the script used to write the books of Enoch, scholars believe they were more popular early on and lost their importance within whichever community was using them, as, even the Aramaic texts use an earlier form of the Aramaic script. The latest any section could date to, based on the script used, is 100 BC, however, most scholars currently suggest a date between 300 and 200 BC is more likely.

Nevertheless, the Semitic Books of Enoch were used by the first Christians, including Jesus' brother Jude, who referenced the Book of the Watchers in the Letter of Jude. There are also references within the Letters of Peter that show Peter viewed them as scripture. The Semitic Books of Enoch were treated as scripture by many early Christian leaders in the era before the Imperial Church was established by Emperor Constantine, including Barnabas, Athenagoras, Clement of Alexandria, Irenaeus, and Tertullian. We know from Tertullian's writings circa 200 AD, that the Jews of his time had rejected the books of Enoch entirely, which is later proven by the fact that the Masoretes never bothered copying them, and they aren't in the Hebrew Bible today. The Semitic books of Enoch did continue to be used by the Israelite community in the Sudan and Ethiopia, which had become generally cut off from the rest of the Jews around 225 BC, and is therefore still used by the Beta Israel community in Ethiopia, Eritrea, and Israeli today.

When the Imperial Church was formed, the church leaders of the day debated for centuries about which books should be in the Bible. The Imperial Church, before the schism between the Latin Catholics and the Greek Orthodox, held seven Ecumenical Councils between 325 and 787 AD to decide which books should be in the Bible. The books of Enoch were only briefly debated in the First Ecumenical Council because Jude, Peter, and Barnabas all treated them as scripture, and the writing of Jude, Peter, and Barnabas were all treated as scripture themselves. They were ultimately not included in Imperial Bibles as they were not part of the Septuagint, the Greek translation of the Hebrew scriptures made at the Library of Alexandria between 250 and 132 BC.

There was quite a lot of debate about Enoch within the early Christian churches before the Imperial Church was formed, and most churches did not use Enoch, largely because of the prediction of the end of the world, which was predicted to come 10,000 years after the time of Enoch. If the text is dated by the reference to the Pleiades being trapped beyond the eastern horizon when the sun rises, then the Book of the Watchers, or part of it, dates back to between 2300 and 2000 BC, meaning the end of the world would take place between 7700 and 8000 AD. This contradicted the general Latin Christian view by the beginning of the 4th century that the end of the world was coming in the year 500 AD. The idea did not have the same support in Greek lands where the Civil calendar was in use, however, in Latin countries where the Anno Mundi calendar was in use, which based its year on when the world was made according to the Septuagint, the year 500 AD, was the year 6000 AM, and, based on various ancient predictions found in Messianic Jewish literature, that was when God was going to return to the Earth and destroy it. Latin Christians were so convinced that the end of the world was coming in 500 AD, that they allowed the Roman empire in the west to collapse in the 4th and 5th centuries, which further fed the belief that it was the end-times. Perhaps if they had have adopted the books of Enoch into their Bibles the Roman Empire would still be around.

Book of the Watchers - Chapter 1

THE WORDS OF THE BLESSING of Enoch, which he blessed the elect and righteous, who will be living in the day of tribulation when all the wicked and godless are to be removed.

He started his parable saying, "Enoch a righteous man, whose eyes were opened by God, saw the vision of the Holy One[W1] in the sky,[W2] which the watchers[W3] showed me, and from them, I heard everything, and from them, I understood as I saw, but not for this generation, but for a remote one which is for to come."

Regarding the chosen, I said, and started my parable concerning them, "The Great Holy One will come out from his home, and the eternal God will tread on the Earth, on Mount Sinai, and appear from his camp and appear in the strength of his might from the sky of the skies. All will be destroyed with fear and the Watchers will tremble and great fear and trembling will seize them to the ends of the Earth. The high mountains will be shaken, and the high hills will be knocked low and will melt like wax before the flame and the Earth will be ripped asunder, and all that is on the Earth will die, and there will be a judgment on all. But with the righteous, he will make peace. Will protect the elect, and will show mercy to them. They will all belong to God, and they will prosper, and they will all be blessed. He will help them all, and light will appear to them, and he will make peace with them. Look! He comes with ten-thousand of his holy ones to execute judgment on all, and to destroy all the ungodly. To convict all flesh of all the works of their ungodliness which they have ungodly committed, and of all the hard things which ungodly sinners have spoken against him."

Book of the Watchers - Chapter 2

[ENOCH CONTINUED,] "SEE everything that takes place in the sky, how their orbits do not change, and the luminaries which are in the sky, how they all rise and set in order, each in its season, and don't change from their appointed order. See the Earth, and pay attention to the things which take place on it from first to last, how steadfast they are, how none of the things on Earth change, but all the works of God appear to you. Look the at summer and the winter, how the whole Earth is filled with water, and clouds and dew and rain cover it."

Book of the Watchers - Chapter 3

[ENOCH CONTINUED,] "OBSERVE and see how all the trees seem as though they have withered and shed all their leaves, except fourteen trees, which do not lose their foliage but retain the old foliage for two to three years until the new grows."

Book of the Watchers - Chapter 4

[ENOCH CONTINUED,] "AGAIN, see the days of summer, how the Sun is above the Earth. You seek shade and shelter because of the heat of the sun, and the Earth also burns with growing heat, and so you cannot tread on the Earth, or on a rock because of its heat."

Book of the Watchers - Chapter 5

[ENOCH CONTINUED,] "SEE how the trees cover themselves with green leaves and grow fruit, which you pay attention and know about all his works, and recognize how he that lives forever has made them so. All his works go on from year to year forever, and all the tasks which they accomplish for him, and their tasks don't change, but as God has ordained, so is it done. See how the sea and the rivers also don't change their tasks from his commandments. But you, you have not been steadfast or done the commandments of the Lord,[W4] but you have turned away and spoken proud and hard words with your impure mouths against his greatness. Oh, you unfeeling, you will find no peace. Therefore will you count your days, and the years of your life will perish, and the years of your destruction will be multiplied in eternal execration. In those days, you will make your names an eternal curse to all the righteous, band by you will all who curse, curse, and all the sinners and godless will imprecate by you."

"For you the godless there will be a curse. All the [... missing text ...] will rejoice, and there will be forgiveness of sins, and every mercy and peace and patience, there will be salvation to them, a goodly light. For all of you sinners, there will be no salvation, but on you, all will live with a curse. But for the elect there will be light and joy and peace, They will inherit the Earth. Then there will be bestowed on the elect wisdom, and they will all live and never again sin, either through ungodliness or through pride. But they who are wise will be humiliated. They will not transgress again, or will they sin all the days of their life, or will they die in anger or rage, but they will complete the number of the days of their life. Their lives will be increased in peace, and the years of their joy will be multiplied, in eternal gladness and peace, all the days of their life."

Book of the Watchers - Chapter 6

IT HAPPENED WHEN THE children of men had multiplied, that in those days, beautiful daughters were born to them. The watchers, the children of the sky, saw and lusted after them, and said to one another, "Come, let us choose wives from among the children of men and father children."

Their leader Samyaza[W5] said to them, "I fear you will not agree to this, and I alone will have to pay the penalty of a great sin."

They all answered him and said, "Let's all swear an oath, and all bind ourselves by mutual curses to not abandon this plan, but to do this."

Then they all swore together and bound themselves by mutual curses to do it. They were two hundred, who descended in the days of Jared to the summit of Mount Hermon,[W6] and they named it Mount Hermon because they had sworn and bound themselves by mutual curses on it. These are the names of their leaders: Samyaza, their leader, Arakiel, Rameel, Kokabiel, Tamiel, Ramiel, Danel,[W7] Chazaqiel, Baraqiel, Azazel, Armaros, Batariel, Ananiel, Zaqiel, Shamsiel, Sathariel, Turiel, Yomiel, and Sariel. These are their chiefs of tens.

Book of the Watchers - Chapter 7

ALL THE OTHERS TOGETHER with them took for themselves wives, and each chose one for himself, and they began to go into them and to defile themselves with them, and they taught them charms and enchantments, and the cutting of roots, and taught them to grow plants. They became pregnant, and they carried great giants, whose height was three thousand[W8] cubits,[W9] who consumed all the property of men. When men could no longer sustain them, the giants turned against them and devoured mankind. They began to eat birds, animals, reptiles, fish, and to devour one another's flesh, and drink their blood. Then the Earth[W10] accused the lawless ones.

Book of the Watchers - Chapter 8

AZAZEL TAUGHT MEN TO make swords, knives, shields, breastplates and taught them about the metals of the Earth and how to work them, as well as bracelets, ornaments, and the use of antimony for beautifying the eyelids, and all kinds of precious gems, and all colorful herbal ointments. Much godlessness took place. They committed fornication and they have led astray and became corrupt in all their ways. Samyaza taught enchantments and root-cuttings. Armaros taught the solution of enchantments. Baraqiel taught astrology and Kokabiel taught the constellations. Chazaqiel taught the knowledge of the clouds. Araqiel taught the signs of the Earth, Shamsiel the signs of the sun, and Sariel the course of the moon. As men died, they cried, and their cry went up to the sky [... missing text ...]

Book of the Watchers - Chapter 9

THEN MICHAEL, URIEL, Raphael, and Gabriel looked down from the sky and saw a great deal of blood being shed on the Earth, and all lawlessness being done on the Earth. They said one to another, "The Earth is being made empty, and cries up to the gates of the sky. Now to you, the holy ones of the sky, the minds[W11] of men make their case, saying, 'Bring our cause before the Highest.'"[W12]

They said to the Lord of the ages, "Lord of lords, God of gods, king of kings, and god of the ages, the throne of your glory stands to all the generations of the ages, and your name holy and glorious and blessed to all the ages! You have made all things, and have power over all things, and all things are naked and open in your sight, and you see all things, and nothing can hide from you. You see what Azazel has done, who has taught all unrighteousness on Earth and revealed the eternal secrets which were in the sky, which men were striving to learn. Samyaza, to whom you have given authority to rule over his associates. They have gone to the daughters of men on the Earth, and have slept with the women, and have defiled themselves, and revealed to them all kinds of sins. The women have given birth to giants, and the whole Earth has been filled with blood and unrighteousness. Now, look, the minds of those who have died are crying and making their case to the gates of the sky, and their lamentations have ascended, and cannot stop because of the lawless deeds which are worked on the Earth. You know all things before they come to pass, and you see these things and you allow them, and you have not told us what we are to do to them because of this."

Book of the Watchers - Chapter 10

———

THEN SAID THE HIGHEST, the holy and great one spoke, and sent Uriel to the son of Lamech, and said to him, "Go to Noah and tell him in my name 'Hide yourself!' and tell him the end that is approaching, and that the whole Earth will be destroyed, and a deluge is about to cover the whole Earth and will destroy all that is on it. Instruct him that he may escape and his seed may be preserved for all the generations of the world."

The Lord said to Raphael, "Tie up Azazel by his hands and feet and throw him into the darkness. Make an opening in the desert, which is in Dudael,[W13] and throw him in there. Place on him rough and jagged rocks, and cover him with darkness, and let him remain there forever, and cover his face that he may not see light. On the day of the great judgment, he will be thrown into the fire. Heal the Earth which the watchers have corrupted, and proclaim the healing of the Earth, that they may heal the plague, and that all the children of men may not die because of all the secret things that the Watchers have disclosed and have taught their sons. The whole Earth has been corrupted through the works that were taught by Azazel, and because of him all sin."

The Lord said to Gabriel, "Move against the bastards and the sinners, and the children of fornication. Destroy the children of fornication and the children of the Watchers from among men, and make them die out. Make them battle against one another that they may destroy each other in battle, so a great length of days will they will not have. Any request that they make of you, will be granted to their fathers on their behalf. They hope to live an eternal life, but each one of them will only live five hundred years."

The Lord said to Michael, "Go, capture Samyaza and his associates who have married women and have defiled themselves with them in all their uncleanness. When their sons have slain one another, and they have seen the destruction of their beloved ones, incarcerate them for seventy generations in the valleys of the Earth until the day of their judgment and their consummation, until the judgment that is forever and ever is consummated. In those days they will be led off to the abyss[W14] of fire, and to the torment and the prison in which they will be confined forever. Whoever will be condemned and destroyed will from that time be bound together with them to the end of all generations. Destroy all the spirits of the sinners and the children of the Watchers, because they have wronged mankind. Destroy all wrong from the face of the Earth and let every evil work come to an end, and let the plant of righteousness and truth appear."

"It will prove a blessing, and the works of righteousness and truth will be planted in truth and joy forever. Then all the righteous will escape, and live until they father thousands of children, and all the days of their youth and their old age will they live in peace. Then the whole Earth will be farmed in righteousness, and will all be planted with trees and be full of blessing. All desirable trees will be planted on it, and they will plant vines on it. The vine which they plant on it will yield wine in abundance, and as for all the seed which is sown on it each measure will carry a thousand, and each measure of olives will yield ten presses of oil. Cleanse the Earth from all oppression, and all unrighteousness, and all sin, and all godlessness, and all the uncleanness that is worked on the Earth will be destroyed from off the Earth. All the children of men will become righteous, and all nations will offer adoration and will praise me, and all will worship me. The Earth will be cleansed from all defilement, and all sin, and all punishment, and all torment, and I will never again send them on it from generation to generation and forever."

Book of the Watchers - Chapter 11

[THE LORD CONTINUED] "In those days I will open the store chambers of blessing which are in the sky, to send them down to the Earth to do the work and labor of the children of men. Truth and peace will be associated together throughout all the days of the world and throughout all the generations of men."

Book of the Watchers - Chapter 12

BEFORE THESE THINGS Enoch was hidden, and none of the children of men knew where he was hidden, and where he lived, and what had become of him. His activities had to do with the Watchers, and his days were with the holy ones.

I, Enoch was praying the Lord of majesty and the king of the ages, and the Watchers called me, "Enoch the scribe," and said to me, "Enoch, you scribe of righteousness, go, tell to the Watchers of the sky who have left the highest sky, the holy eternal place, and have defiled themselves with women, and have done as the children of Earth do, and have taken for themselves wives, 'You have worked great destruction on the Earth. You will have no peace or forgiveness of sin,' and in as much as they delight themselves in their children, the murder of their beloved ones will they see, and will they lament over the destruction of their children, and will make supplication to eternity, 'but mercy and peace will you not receive.'"

Book of the Watchers - Chapter 13

ENOCH WENT, AND SAID, "Azazel, you will have no peace. A terrible sentence has been made against you, to put you in bonds. You will not be tolerated, nor will requests be granted for you, because of the unrighteousness that you have taught, and because of all the works of godlessness and unrighteousness and sin which you have shown to men."

Then, I went and spoke to them all together, and they were all afraid, and fear and trembling seized them. They begged me to write a petition for them that they might find forgiveness and to read their petition in the presence of the lord of the sky. As from then onward they could not speak (with him) or lift up their eyes to the sky because of the shame of their sins for which they had been condemned. So I wrote down their petition, and individual prayers about their spirits, regarding their deeds and their request that they should be forgiven and given a length of days. I went off and sat down at the waters of Dan, in the land of Dan, to the south of the west of Hermon, and I read their petition until I fell asleep.

I saw a dream came over me, and visions came down to me. I saw visions of punishment, and a voice told me to tell the sons of the sky about it, and reprimand them. When I awoke, I went to them, and they were all sitting gathered together, weeping in the meadow of waters,[W15] which is between Lebanon and Sirion,[W16] with their faces covered. I retold them all the visions which I had seen in my sleep, and I told them the words of righteousness, and I reprimanded the heavenly Watchers.

Book of the Watchers - Chapter 14

THE BOOK OF THE RIGHTEOUS words, and the reprimand of the eternal Watchers by the command of the great Holy One in that vision.

"I will not state what I saw in my sleep, with a tongue of flesh and the breath of my mouth, which the great one has given men to speak with and understand with the heart. As he created and gave man the power of understanding the word of wisdom, so he created me also and given me the power to reprimand the Watchers, the children of the sky."

"I wrote down your petition, and in my vision, it appeared that your petition will not be granted to you throughout all of eternity, and that judgment has been finally passed on you. Your petition will not be granted to you. From now on you will not ascend into the sky for all eternity, and in bonds of the Earth the decree has gone out to bind you for all the days of the world. You will see the destruction of your beloved sons and you will have no pleasure in them, but they will fall before you by the sword. Your petition on their behalf will not be granted, not even for you. Even if you cry and pray and speak all the words contained in the writing which I have written."

"This is the vision I saw. In the vision, clouds invited me and a mist summoned me, and the course of the stars and the lightning speed up, and the winds in the vision caused me to fly and lifted me upward, and carried me into the sky. I went in until I approached a wall which is built of crystals and surrounded by tongues of fire, and it scared me. I went into the tongues of fire and approached a large house which was built of crystals, and the walls of the house were like a tessellated floor made of crystals, and its foundation was of crystal. Its ceiling was like the path of the stars and the lightning, and between them were fiery cherubs,[W17] and their the sky was water. A flaming fire surrounded the walls, and its doorway blazed with fire."

"I entered into that house, and it was hot as fire and cold as ice. There were no delights of life within it, and fear filled me, and trembling took hold of me. I quaked and trembled. I fell to my face, and I saw another vision. There was a second house, greater than the first, and the entire doorway stood open before me, and it was built of flames of fire. It was so magnificent and majestic that I cannot describe it to you. Its floor was of fire, and above it were lightnings and the path of the stars, and its ceiling also was flaming fire."

"I looked and saw within a lofty throne. Its looked like a crystal wheel bright as the sun, and there was the vision of cherubs. From underneath the throne came streams of flaming fire so bright that I could not look at it. The great glory sat on it, and his clothing shone more brightly than the sun and was whiter than any snow. None of the watchers could enter or look his face because of the magnificence and glory and no flesh could look him. The flaming fire was around him, and a great fire stood before him, and none around could draw near him. One hundred million stood before him, yet he needed no counselor. The holy ones who were near him did not leave either by night or by day."

Until then, I had been prostrate on my face, trembling, and the lord called me with his own mouth, and said to me, "Come here, Enoch, and hear my words."

One of the holy ones came to me and woke me, and he told me to get up and approach the door, and I bowed my face downward.

Book of the Watchers - Chapter 15

HE ANSWERED ME, AND I heard his voice, "Don't be afraid, Enoch, you righteous man and scribe of righteousness. Approach and hear my voice. Go and say to the Watchers of the sky, who has sent you to intercede for them. "You should intercede for men, and not men for you. Why have you left the high holy and eternal the sky, and laid with women, and defiled yourselves with the daughters of men and taken for yourselves wives, and done like the children of Earth, and begotten giant sons? Though you were holy, spiritual, and living the eternal life, you have defiled yourselves with the blood of women, and have begotten the blood of flesh, and, as the children of men, have lusted after flesh and blood as those also do who die."

"Therefore, you have taken them as wives, so that you might impregnate them, and father children by them, that therefore nothing might be lacking for them on Earth. But you were formerly spiritual, living the eternal life, and immortal for all generations of the world. But I have not appointed wives for you, and for as for the spiritual ones of the sky, in the sky is their home. From now on, the giants, who have been produced from the spirits and flesh, will be called evil spirits on the Earth, and on the Earth will be their home. Evil spirits have come from their bodies, because they are born from men, but from the holy ones was their beginning and primal origin. They will be evil spirits on Earth, and they will be known as evil spirits. As for the spirits of the sky, in the sky will be their home, but as for the spirits of the Earth which were born on the Earth, on the Earth will be their home. The spirits of the giants afflict, oppress, destroy, attack, battle, and work destruction on the Earth, and cause trouble. They eat no food, but nevertheless hunger and thirst, and cause offenses. These spirits will rise up against the children of men and against the women, because they have come from them."

Book of the Watchers - Chapter 16

[ENOCH CONTINUED,] "FROM the days of the slaughter, destruction, and death of the giants, the spirits having gone come from the minds of their flesh, and will destroy without judgment, so will they continue until the day of the consummation, the great judgment in which the age will be consummated. Even the Watchers and the godless, you will be completely consummated."

"Now as to the Watchers who have sent you to intercede for them, who had been previously in the sky, [say to them,] 'You have been in the sky, but all the mysteries had not yet been revealed to you, and you knew minor ones, and these due to the hardness of your hearts you have made known to women, and through these mysteries, women and men work much evil on Earth.' Say to them, 'You have no peace.'"

Book of the Watchers - Chapter 17

THEY TOOK ME TO A PLACE where those who were there looked like a flaming fire, but when they wanted to could look like men. They took me to the place of darkness, and to a mountain with a summit that reached the sky. I saw the places of the luminaries and the vault of the stars and the thunder and in the farthest depths, where there was a fiery bow and arrows and their quiver, and a fiery sword and all the lightning. They took me to the living waters, and to the fire of the west, which receives every setting of the sun. I came to a river of fire in which the fire flows like water and discharges itself into the great sea towards the west. I saw the great rivers and came to the great darkness, and went to the place where no flesh walks. I saw the mountains of the darkness of winter and the place where all the waters of the deep flow. I saw the mouths of all the rivers of the Earth and the mouth of the deep.

Book of the Watchers - Chapter 18

I SAW THE VAULT OF all the winds, and I saw how he had furnished with them the whole creation and the firm foundations of the Earth. I saw the corner-stone of the Earth, and I saw the four winds which carry the Earth and the firmament of the sky. I saw how the winds stretch out the vaults of the sky and have their station between the sky and Earth. These are the pillars of the sky. I saw the winds of the sky which turn and bring the circumference of the Sun and all the stars to their setting. I saw the winds on the Earth carrying the clouds. I saw the paths of the watchers. I saw at the edge of the Earth the firmament of the sky above.

I continued on, and saw a place that burns day and night, where there are seven mountains of magnificent stones, three to the east, and three to the south. As for those to the east, one was of colored stone, and one of pearl, and one of jacinth,[W18] and those to the south were of red stone. But the middle one which reached to the sky like the throne of God, was of alabaster, and the summit of the throne was of sapphire. I saw a flaming fire.

Beyond these mountains is a region the edge of the great Earth. There the skies were completed. I saw a deep abyss, with columns of heavenly fire, and among them I saw columns of fire fall, which were beyond measure both in their height and in their depth. Beyond that abyss I saw a place which had no firmament of the sky above, and no firmly founded Earth beneath it. There was no water on it, and no birds, but it was a waste and horrible place. I saw there seven stars like great burning mountains, and to me, when I asking about them, the watcher answered, "This place is the end of the Sky and Earth. This has become a prison for the stars and the armies of the sky. The stars which roll over the fire are they which have transgressed the commandment of the Lord in the beginning of their rising, because they did not come out at their appointed times.[W19] He was angry with them, and bound them for ten thousand years, until the time when their guilt would be consummated."[W20]

Book of the Watchers - Chapter 19

URIEL TOLD ME, "THE watchers who have connected themselves with women will remain here. Their spirits assume many different forms and are defiling mankind, and leading them astray into sacrificing to demons as gods, will stay here until the day of the great judgment when they will be judged and their end will come. The women also of the watchers who went astray will become sirens."[W21]

I, Enoch, alone saw the vision of the ends of all things, and no man will see what I have seen.

Book of the Watchers - Chapter 20

THESE ARE THE NAMES of the holy ones who watch.

Uriel, one of the holy ones, who watches over the world and also Tartarus.[W22]

Raphael, one of the holy ones, who watches over the spirits of men.

Deuel, one of the holy ones who takes vengeance on the world of the luminaries.

Michael, one of the holy ones, who watches over the best part of mankind and over chaos.[W23]

Saraqael, one of the holy ones, who watches over the spirits that sin in the spirit.

Gabriel, one of the holy ones, who watches over Paradise[W24] and the Seraphs[W25] and Cherubs.

Remiel, one of the holy ones, who God set to watch over those who rise.

Book of the Watchers - Chapter 21

I CONTINUED TO WHERE things were chaotic, and I saw there something horrible. I saw neither the sky above or a firm land below, but a place that was chaotic and horrible. There, I saw seven stars of the sky, bound together in it like great mountains and burning with fire.

I asked, "What sin are they bound for? On what account have they been thrown in here?"

Uriel, one of the holy ones, who was with me, and was chief over them, and answered, "Enoch, why do you ask, and why are you eager for the truth? These are of the number of the stars of the sky, who have transgressed the commandments of the Lord, and are bound here for ten thousand years until the time prescribed by their sins are completed."

From there, I went to another place which was even more horrible than the former, where I saw a horrible thing. A great fire burned and blazed there, and the place was split as far as the abyss, full of great descending columns of fire. I could not see the end of them, either in distance or in depth. I said, "How terrible is this place and how awful to look at!"

Uriel, one of the holy ones who was with me, replied to me, "Enoch, why have you become so afraid?"

I answered, "Because of this terrible place, and the horror I see."

He said to me, "This is the prison of the watchers, and here they will be imprisoned forever."

Book of the Watchers - Chapter 22

AFTER THAT, I WENT to another place, and he showed me another great and high mountain of hard rock in the west. There were four hollow places in it, deep and very smooth. Three of them were dark and one bright, and there was a fountain of water in its middle.

I asked, "How smooth are these hollow places? And how deep is the darkness I see."

Then Raphael, one of the holy ones who was with me, and answered me, "These hollow places have been created so the spirits of the minds of the dead should assemble there. So all the minds of the children of men should assemble here. These places have been made to receive them until the day of their judgment and until their appointed time until the appointed time of the great judgment of them."

I saw the spirits of the children of men who were dead, and their voices went up to the sky and made claims. He answered me, "This is the spirit which came out from Abel, who his brother Cain killed, and he makes his claim against him until his descendants are destroyed from the face of the Earth, and his seed is annihilated from among the descendants of men."

Then I asked about it, and about all the hollow places, "Why is one separated from the other?"

He answered, "These three have been made so that the spirits of the dead might be separated. The division has been made for the spirits of the righteous, which are there in the bright spring of water. This has been made for sinners when they die and are buried in the Earth and judgment has not been executed on them in their lifetime. Here, their spirits will be set apart in great pain until the great day of judgment and punishment and torment of those who curse forever, and retribution for their spirits. There he will bind them forever. Such a division has been made for the spirits of those who make their case, who make disclosures about their destruction when they were slain in the days of the sinners. This has been made for the spirits of men who will not be righteous but sinners, who are godless, and of the lawless, they will be companions. Their spirits will not be punished in the day of judgment or will they be raised from there."

Then I blessed the Lord of Glory[W32] and said, "Blessed are you, Lord of righteousness, who rules over the world."

Book of the Watchers - Chapter 23

FROM THERE I WENT TO another place to the west of the edge of the Earth, where I saw a burning fire that continued without stopping, and did not pause its course day or night but continued constantly.

I asked, "What is this, which does not rest?"

Then Deuel, one of the holy ones who was with me, answered me and said to me, "This course of fire which you have seen is the fire in the west which persecutes all the luminaries of the sky."

Book of the Watchers - Chapter 24

FROM THERE I WENT TO another place on the Earth, and he showed me a mountain range of fire which burnt day and night. I went beyond it and saw seven magnificent mountains all differing each from the other, and the stones were magnificent and beautiful, glorious in appearance and beautiful. Three to the east, one founded on the other, and three towards the south, one on the other, with deep rough ravines which did not connect to each other.

The seventh mountain was among these, and it was higher, resembling the seat of a throne, with fragrant trees surrounding the throne. Among them was a tree that I had never smelled before. It was the only one like it among them and had a greater odor that all other fragrance. Its leaves and blooms and wood did not wither forever, and its fruit is beautiful resembling the dates of a palm.

I stated, "What is this beautiful tree, so fragrant, and its leaves are beautiful, with such very delightful flowers."

Michael, one of the holy and honored watchers who was with me, and was their leader [continued in the next chapter]

Book of the Watchers - Chapter 25

[CONTINUED FROM THE last chapter] said to me, "Enoch, why do you ask me about the fragrance of the tree, and why do you wish to learn the truth?"

Then I answered him, "I want to know about everything, but especially about this tree."

He answered, "This high mountain which you have seen, whose summit is like the throne of God, is his throne, where the great Holy One, the Lord of Glory, the Eternal King, will sit when he comes down to visit the Earth with goodness. As for this fragrant tree, no mortal is permitted to touch it until the great judgment, when he will take vengeance on all and finalize everything forever. It will then be given to the righteous and holy. Its fruit will be for food to the chosen, and it will be transplanted to the holy place, to the temple of the Lord, the Eternal King.

Then will they rejoice and celebrate, and into the holy place will they enter. Its fragrance will be in their bones, and they will live a long life on Earth, like your fathers lived. In their days will no sorrow or plague or torment or calamity touch them."

Then blessed I the God of Glory, the Eternal King, who has prepared such things for the righteous, and have created them and promised to give to them.

Book of the Watchers - Chapter 26

I WENT FROM THERE TO the middle of the Earth,[W26] and I saw a blessed place where were trees with branches living and blooming from a dismembered tree. There, I saw a holy mountain, and underneath the mountain, to the east, there was a stream flowing towards the south. I saw towards the east another mountain higher than this and between them a deep and narrow ravine. In it, a stream also ran underneath the mountain. To the west of there was another mountain, lower than the former and of small elevation, and a deep, dry ravine between them, and another deep, dry ravine was at the extremities of the three mountains. All the ravines were deep and narrow and made from hard rock, and there were no trees in them. I marveled at the rocks, and I marveled at the ravine. I marveled greatly.

Book of the Watchers - Chapter 27

THEN I ASKED, "FOR what reason is this land blessed, which is completely filled with trees, and this valley in between cursed?"

Uriel, one of the holy ones who was with me, answered and said, "This cursed valley is for those who are cursed forever. Here all the cursed will be gathered together who speak evil words against the Lord, and terrible things about his glory. Here they will be gathered together, and here will be the place where they remain. In the last days, there will be a spectacle of righteous judgment in the presence of the righteous forever. Here the merciful will bless the Lord of glory, the Eternal King. In the days of judgment over the former, they will bless him for the mercy by which he has assigned them."

Then I blessed the Lord of Glory and set out his glory and praised him gloriously.

Book of the Watchers - Chapter 28

THEN I WENT TO THE east, to the middle of the mountain range of the desert, and I saw a wilderness that was isolated but full of trees and plants. Water gushed out from above, rushing like a torrential river that flowed towards the north-west, and caused clouds and dew to rise on every side.

Book of the Watchers - Chapter 29

THEN I WENT TO ANOTHER place in the desert, to the east of this mountain range. I saw aromatic trees there, which smelled the fragrance of frankincense and myrrh, and the trees also were similar to the almond tree.

Book of the Watchers - Chapter 30

BEYOND THESE, I WENT further to the east, and I saw another place, a valley of water. There was a tree within it the color of the fragrant trees such as the mastic.[W27] On the sides of those valleys, I saw fragrant cinnamon. Beyond this, I continued to the east.

Book of the Watchers - Chapter 31

I SAW OTHER MOUNTAINS, and among them were groves of trees, and nectar flowed out from them, which are named styrax and galbanum.[W28] Beyond these mountains, I saw another mountain farther east to the edge of the Earth, where were aloe trees and all the trees were full of stacte,[W29] being like almond-trees. When one burnt it, it smelt sweeter than any fragrant odor.

Book of the Watchers - Chapter 32

AFTER THESE FRAGRANT odors, as I looked towards the north over the mountains I saw seven mountains full of beautiful flowers and fragrant trees and cinnamon and pepper. I went there, over the summits of all these mountains, far towards the east of the Earth, and passed above the Erythraean sea and went far from it, and passed over the watcher Zotiel.[W30] I came to the Garden of Righteousness and saw from far away more numerous trees than the trees here,[W31] and saw two great trees there, extremely great, beautiful and glorious, and magnificent. One was the tree of knowledge, whose holy fruit they eat and know great wisdom. That tree is at tall as the fir, and its leaves are like the Carob tree, and its fruit is very beautiful like the clusters of the vine, and the fragrance of the tree traveled great distances.

I said, "What is this beautiful tree that is so beautiful is its to see!"

Then Raphael the holy one, who was with me, answered me, "This is the tree of wisdom, of which your fore-father and your ancestral mother, who were before you, ate, and they learned wisdom. Their eyes were opened and they knew that they were naked and they were driven out of the garden."

Book of the Watchers - Chapter 33

FROM THERE, I WENT to the edge of the Earth and saw great beasts there, each differed from the other, and also birds which differed in appearance, beauty, and voice, each differing from the other. To the east of those beasts I saw the edge of the Earth on which the sky rests, and the portals of the sky open. I saw how the stars of the sky come out, and I counted the portals out of which they come, and wrote down all their portals of each star by itself, according to their number and their names, their courses and their positions, and their times and their months, as Uriel the holy one who was with me showed me. He showed all things to me and wrote them down for me. Also their names he wrote for me, and their laws and their groupings.

Book of the Watchers - Chapter 34

FROM THERE, I WENT to the north to the edge of the Earth, and I saw there a great and glorious device at the edge of the whole Earth. Here I saw three portals of the sky open in the sky. Through each of them proceed north winds, and when they blow there is cold, hail, frost, snow, dew, and rain. Out of one portal they blow for good, but when they blow through the other two portals, it is with violence and affliction on the Earth, and they blow with violence.

Book of the Watchers - Chapter 35

FROM THERE, I WENT to the west to the edge of the Earth and saw there three portals of the sky open like as I had seen in the east, the same number of portals, and the same number of openings.

Book of the Watchers - Chapter 36

FROM THERE, I WENT to the south to the edge of the Earth and saw there three open portals of the sky, and from there come dew, rain, and wind.

From there, I went to the east to the edge of the sky and saw there the three eastern portals of the sky open and small portals above them. Through each of these small portals passed the stars of the sky to run their course to the west along a path which is shown to them.

As I saw each one, I blessed always the Lord of Glory, and I continued to bless the Lord of Glory who has worked great and glorious wonders, to show the greatness of his work to the watchers and spirits and men, that they might praise his work and all his creation, and that they might see the work of his might and praise the great work of his hands and bless him forever.

Book of Parables - Chapter 1

THE SECOND VISION WHICH he saw, the vision of wisdom, seen by Enoch the son of Jared, the son of Mahalalel, the son of Kenan, the son of Enos, the son of Seth, the son of Adam.

This is the beginning of the words of wisdom, which I rose my voice to speak, and tell to those who live on Earth. You men of ancient times, and those that come later, listen to the words of the Holy One[P1] which I will state before the Lord of Spirit.[P2] In ancient times it was better to only tell the men, but form those that come later, we will not withhold this wisdom. Until today, wisdom like this has never been given by the Lord of Spirit as I have received in my vision. By the great beneficence of the Lord of Spirit, I also received the fate of eternal life.

Now three parables were told to me, and I lifted my voice and retold them to those that live on the Earth.

Book of Parables - Chapter 2

THE FIRST PARABLE.

When the congregation of the righteous will appear, and sinners will be judged for their sins and will be driven off the face of the Earth when the Righteous One will appear before the eyes of the righteous, whose special works depend on the Lord of Spirit, and lights will appear to the righteous and the chosen who live on the Earth, where will the sinners live then? Where will be the resting-place of those who have denied the Lord of Spirit? It would be better for them if they had not been born.

When the secrets of the righteous will be revealed, the sinners judged and the godless driven from the presence of the righteous and chosen, from that time those that possess the Earth will no longer be powerful and exalted. They will not be able to look the face of the holy, for the Lord of Spirit will have caused his light to appear in the faces of the holy, righteous, and chosen.

Then the kings and mighty will perish and be given into the hands of the righteous and holy. From then on, none will seek for themselves mercy from the Lord of Spirit for their life will have ended.

Book of Parables - Chapter 3

"IT WILL HAPPEN IN THOSE days, that the chosen and holy children will descend from the high the sky, and their seed will become one with the children of men, like in the days Enoch received books of zeal and anger and books of the disturbance and expulsion. Mercy will not be accorded to them," said the Lord of Spirit.

In those days, a flying-wheel[P3] carried me up from the Earth and set me down at the limits of the sky.

There, I saw another vision, the living-places of the holy, and the resting-places of the righteous.

My eyes saw there the homes of the righteous watchers, and their resting-places of the holy. They petitioned and interceded and prayed for the children of men, and righteousness flowed from them like water and mercy like the dew on the Earth. It is like this among them forever and ever. In that place, my eyes saw the chosen one of righteousness and the faithful, and I saw his living-place under the wings of the Lord of Spirit. Righteousness will prevail in his days, and the righteous and chosen will be without number before him forever and ever. All the righteous and chosen before him will be as strong as fiery lights, and their mouth will be full of blessing, and their lips will praise the name of the Lord of Spirit, and righteousness before him will never fail, and uprightness will never fail before him. I wished to live there, and my spirit longed for that living-place. Therefore this was granted to me, as the Lord of Spirit has established it for me.

In those days I praised the name of the Lord of Spirit with blessings and praises because he has destined me to bless and praise him. For a long time, my eyes saw that place, and I blessed him and praised him, saying, "Blessed is he, and may he be blessed from the beginning and forever. Before him, there is no end. He knows before the world was created what will happen forever, and what will happen from generation to generation. Those who don't sleep bless you, and they stand before your glory and bless, praise, and extol, saying, 'Holy, holy, holy, is the Lord of Spirit. He filled the Earth with spirits.'"

Here my eyes saw all those who do not sleep. They stand before him and bless and say, "Blessed are you, and blessed is the name of the Lord forever and ever."

My face was changed, and I could no longer look.

Book of Parables - Chapter 4

THEN I SAW THOUSANDS of thousands and ten thousand times ten thousand, I saw a multitude beyond count and reckoning, who stood before the Lord of Spirit. On the four sides of the Lord of Spirit, I saw four beings different from those that don't sleep, and I learned their names, as the watcher that traveled with me told me their names, and showed me all the hidden things. I heard the voices of those four beings as they spoke praises before the Lord of Glory.[P41] The first voice will bless the Lord of Spirit forever and ever. The second voice I heard blessing the chosen one and the chosen ones who hang on the Lord of Spirit. The third voice I heard praying and interceding for those who live on the Earth and supplicate in the name of the Lord of Spirit. I heard the fourth voice fending off the Satans[P4] and forbidding them to come before the Lord of Spirit to accuse those who live on the Earth.

Then I asked the peaceful watcher who traveled with me, who explained to me everything that is hidden, "Who are these four beings that I have seen and whose words I have heard and written down?"

He explained to me, "The first is Michael, the merciful and patient. The second, who is placed over all the diseases and all the wounds of the children of men, is Raphael. The third, who is placed over all the powers, is Gabriel. The fourth, who is placed over the repentance to hope of those who inherit eternal life, is named Penuel."

These are the four watchers of the Lord of Spirit and the four voices I heard in those days.

Book of Parables - Chapter 5

THEN I SAW ALL THE secrets of the skies, and how the kingdom is divided, and how the actions of men are weighed in the balance. There I saw the palaces of the chosen and the palaces of the holy, and my eyes saw there all the sinners being driven away from there, and those who deny the name of the Lord of Spirit and being dragged off, and they could not live because of the punishment which proceeds from the Lord of Spirit.

There, my eyes saw the secrets of the lightning and thunder, and the secrets of the winds, how they are divided to blow over the Earth, and the secrets of the clouds and dew. And there, I saw from where they left from that place, and from where they saturate the dusty Earth. I saw there closed chambers from which the winds are divided, the chambers of the hail, winds, mist, and clouds, and the cloud that hovered over the Earth from the beginning of the world.

I saw the chambers of the sun[P5] and moon,[P6] from where they proceeded and to where they went to, and their glorious view and how one is superior to the other, and their stately orbit, and how they do not leave their orbit, and they add nothing to their orbit and they take nothing from it, and they keep their relationship with each other, in accordance with the oath by which they are bound together. First the sun goes out and traverses his path according to the commandment of the Lord of Spirit, and mighty is his name forever and ever. After that I saw the hidden and the visible path of the moon, and she finishes the course of her path in that place by day and by night, the one holding a position opposite to the other before the Lord of Spirit.

They give thanks and praise and did not rest, a for them is their thanksgiving is rest. The sun does not change either for a blessing or a curse, and the course of the path of the moon is light to the righteous and darkness to the sinners in the name of the Lord, who made a separation between the light and the darkness, and divided the spirits of men, and strengthened the spirits of the righteous, in the name of his righteousness. For no watcher delays him and no power is able to delay him, for he appoints a judge for them all and he judges them all before him.

Book of Parables - Chapter 6

WISDOM[P7] found no place where she might live. Then a living-place was assigned her in the skies. Wisdom went out to make her living among the children of men and found no living-place. Wisdom returned to her place and took her seat among the watchers.

Unrighteousness went out from her chambers. Whoever she did not want, she found and stayed with them, like rain in a desert or dew on a thirsty land.

Book of Parables - Chapter 7

I SAW MORE LIGHTNING and stars in the sky, and I saw him call them all by their names and they listened to him. I saw how they are weighed in a righteous balance according to their proportions of light, the width of their spaces and the day of their appearance, and how their revolution produces lightning, and their revolution according to the number of the watchers, and how they kept in station with each other.

I asked the watcher who went with me who showed me what was hidden, "What are these?"

He said to me, "The Lord of Spirit has shown you their parabolic meaning. These are the names of the holy who live on the Earth and believe in the name of the Lord of Spirit forever and ever."

Book of Parables - Chapter 8

ALSO, I SAW ANOTHER phenomenon regarding the lightning, and how some of the stars rise and become lightning and change from their new form.

Book of Parables - Chapter 9

———

THIS IS THE SECOND Parable, concerning those who deny the name of the living, of the holy ones, and the Lord of Spirit.

They will not ascend into the sky, and they will not return to the Earth. This will be the fate of the sinners who have denied the name of the Lord of Spirit, who are therefore preserved for the day of punishment and tribulation. On that day the chosen one will sit on the throne of glory and will judge their works, and their places of rest will be innumerable. Their minds will grow strong within them when they see the elect ones, and those who have called on the glorious name. Then, will I cause my chosen one to live among them. I will transform the sky and make it an eternal blessing and light and I will transform the Earth and make it a blessing. I will cause my chosen ones to live on it, but the sinners and evil-doers will not set foot on it.

I will provide and satisfy my righteous ones with peace and have caused them to live before me. But, there is a judgment of the sinners coming from me, that I will destroy them from the face of the Earth.

Book of Parables - Chapter 10

I SAW THERE ONE WHO had a head of days,[P8] and his hair was white like wool, and with him was another being who looked like a man, and his face was full of glory, like one of the holy watchers. I asked the watcher who went with me and showed me all the hidden things, concerning that son of Adam,[P9] who he was, and where he was from, and why he had a head of days?

He answered and said to me, "This is the son of Adam who is righteousness, who lived in righteousness, and who revealed all the treasures of that which is hidden, because the Lord of Spirit has chosen him, and whose fate is pre-eminent before the Lord of Spirit in uprightness for ever. This son of Adam who you have seen will overthrow the kings and the mighty from their thrones, and the strong from their thrones and will loosen the reins of the strong, and break the teeth of the sinners. He will throw down the kings from their thrones and kingdoms because they do not praise him, or humbly acknowledge from where their kingdom was bestowed on them. He will overthrow the pride of the strong and will fill them with shame. Darkness will be their home, and worms will be their bed, and they will have no hope of rising from their beds because they do not praise the name of the Lord of Spirit. These are they who judge the stars of the sky, and raise their hands against the Highest and walk on the Earth and live on it. All their deeds show unrighteousness, and their power rests in their riches, and their faith is in the gods which they have made with their hands, and they deny the name of the Lord of Spirit, and they persecute the houses of his congregations, and the faithful who hang on the name of the Lord of Spirit."

Book of Parables - Chapter 11

IN THOSE DAYS, THE prayers of the righteous will had ascended, as well as the blood of the righteous of the Earth before the Lord of Spirit. In those days, the holy ones who live above in the skies unites with one voice and supplicated and prayed and praised and gave thanks and bless the name of the Lord of Spirit on behalf of the blood of the righteous which has been spilled, and that the prayer of the righteous may not be in vain before the Lord of Spirit, that judgment may be done to them, and that they may not have to allow forever.

In those days, I saw the head of days when he seated himself on the throne of his glory, and the books of the living were opened before him. All his army which is in the sky above and his counselors stood before him. The hearts of the holy were filled with joy, because the number of the righteous had been offered, and the prayer of the righteous had been heard, and the blood of the righteous been required before the Lord of Spirit.

Book of Parables - Chapter 12

IN THAT PLACE, I SAW the fountain of righteousness which was never-ending. Around it, were many fountains of wisdom, and all the thirsty drank of them and were filled with wisdom, and their homes were with the righteous and holy and elect. At that hour that son of Adam was named in the presence of the Lord of Spirit, and his name before the head of days.

Yes, before the sun and the constellations were created, before the stars of the sky were made, his name was named before the Lord of Spirit. He will be a staff to the righteous on which to stay themselves and not fall, and he will be the light of the Gentiles, and the hope of those who are troubled of heart. All who live on Earth will fall down and worship before him, and will praise and bless and celebrate with song the Lord of Spirit. For this reason, has he been elect and hidden before Him, before the creation of the world and forever. The wisdom of the Lord of Spirit has revealed him to the holy and righteous, for he has preserved the fate of the righteous, because they have hated and despised this world of unrighteousness, and have hated all its works and ways in the name of the Lord of Spirit. In his name, they are saved, and according to his good pleasure has it been regarding their life.

In these days, the kings of the Earth will have become depressed, as the strong who possess the land because of the works of their hands. For, on the day of their anguish and affliction they will not save themselves. I will give them over into the hands of my chosen, like straws in the fire they burn before the face of the holy. Like lead in the water will they sink before the face of the righteous, and no trace of them will anymore be found.

On the day of their affliction, there will be peace on the Earth, and those before them they will fall and not rise again. There will be none to take them with his hands and raise them, for they have denied the Lord of Spirit and his anointed.

Blessed be the name of the Lord of Spirit, [continued in the next chapter]

Book of Parables - Chapter 13

[CONTINUATION OF THE last chapter] as wisdom is poured out like water, and glory does not fail before him forever. He is mighty in all the secrets of righteousness, and unrighteousness will disappear as a shadow and have no continuance. Because the chosen one stands before the Lord of Spirit, and his glory is forever, and his might for all generations.

In him dwells the spirit of wisdom, and the spirit which gives insight, and the spirit of understanding and might, and the spirit of those who have fallen asleep in righteousness. He will judge the secret things, and none will be able to speak a dishonest word before him. He is the chosen one before the Lord of Spirit according to his good pleasure.

Book of Parables - Chapter 14

IN THOSE DAYS A CHANGE will take place for the holy and elect, and the light of days will live in them, and glory and honor will turn to the holy, on the day of affliction on which evil has been treasured up against the sinners. The righteous will be victorious in the name of the Lord of Spirit. He will cause the others to witness that they may repent and forgo the works of their hands.

They have no honor through the name of the Lord of Spirit, yet, through his name will they be saved, and the Lord of Spirit has compassion on them, for his compassion is great. He is righteous also in his judgment, and in the presence of his glory unrighteousness also will not maintain itself. At his judgment, the unrepentant will perish before him.

"From now on, I will have no mercy on them," said the Lord of Spirit.

Book of Parables - Chapter 15

IN THOSE DAYS, THE Earth will also give back that which has been entrusted to it, and Sheol[P10] also will give back that which it has received, and Hades will give back that which it owes. For in those days the chosen one will rise, he will choose the righteous and holy from among them. For the day has drawn near that they should be saved. The chosen one will in those days sit on my throne, and his mouth will pour out all the secrets of wisdom and counsel. The Lord of Spirit has given to him and has glorified him. In those days, the mountains will leap like rams, and the hills also will skip like lambs satisfied with milk, and the faces of all the watchers in the sky will be lighted up with joy. The Earth will rejoice, and the righteous will live on it, and the chosen will walk on it.

Book of Parables - Chapter 16

AFTER THOSE DAYS, IN that place where I had seen all the visions of that which is hidden after I had been carried off in a flying-wheel and they had taken me to the west. There my eyes saw all the secret things of the sky that will be: a mountain of iron, a mountain of copper, a mountain of silver, a mountain of gold, a mountain of soft metal, and a mountain of lead.

I asked the watcher who went with me, "What things are these which I have seen in secret?"

He answered me, "All these things which you have seen will serve the dominion of his chosen that he may be rich and mighty on the Earth."

The peaceful watcher continued, "Wait a while, and all the secret things which surround the Lord of Spirit will be revealed to you. These mountains which your eyes have seen, the mountain of iron, the mountain of copper, the mountain of silver, the mountain of gold, the mountain of soft metal, and the mountain of lead, all these will be in the presence of the chosen one like wax before the fire, and like the water which streams down from above on those mountains, and they will become powerless before his feet. It will happen in those days that none will be saved, either by gold or by silver, and none be able to escape. There will be no iron for war, and none will clothe himself with a breastplate. Bronze will be of no service, and tin will be of no service and will not be valued, and lead will not be desired. All these things will be denied and destroyed from the surface of the Earth when the chosen one will appear before the face of the Lord of Spirit."

Book of Parables - Chapter 17

THEN MY EYES SAW A deep valley with open mouths, and all who live on the Earth and in the sea and on islands will bring to him gifts and presents and tokens of homage, but that deep valley will never fill up. Their hands will commit lawless deeds, and the sinners will consume all they oppress lawlessly. Yet the sinners will be destroyed from before the face of the Lord of Spirit, and they will be banished from off the face of his Earth, and they will stay dead forever and ever.

I saw all the watchers of punishment staying there and preparing all the instruments of the Satans. I asked the peaceful watcher who went with me, "Who are they preparing these instruments for?"

He answered me, "They prepare these for the kings and the mighty of this Earth, that they may be destroyed with them. After this the Righteous and chosen one will cause the house of his congregation to appear, from now on they will no longer be hindered in the name of the Lord of Spirit. These mountains will not stand like the Earth before his righteousness, but the hills will be like a fountain of water, and the righteous will have peace from the oppression of sinners."

Book of Parables - Chapter 18

I LOOKED AND TURNED to another part of the Earth, and saw there a deep valley with burning fire, where they brought the kings and the mighty, and began to throw them into this deep valley. There, my eyes saw how they made these their instruments, iron chains of immeasurable weight.

I asked the peaceful watcher who went with me, "Who are these chains being prepared for?"

He answered, "These are being prepared for the armies of Azazel, so that they may take them and throw them into the abyss of complete condemnation, and they will cover their jaws with rough stones as the Lord of Spirit commanded. Michael, Gabriel, Raphael, and Penuel will take hold of them on that great day, and on that day throw them into the burning furnace, that the Lord of Spirit may take vengeance on them for their unrighteousness in becoming subject to Satan and leading astray those who live on the Earth."

"In those days punishment will come from the Lord of Spirit, and he will open all the chambers of waters which are above the skies, and of the fountains which are beneath the Earth. All the waters will mix. That which is above the skies is the masculine, and the water which is beneath the Earth is the feminine.[P11] They will destroy all who live on the Earth and those who live under the ends of the sky. When they have recognized their unrighteousness which they have worked on the Earth, then though these they will die."

Book of Parables - Chapter 19

AFTER THAT, THE HEAD of Days repented and said, "I have destroyed all who live on the Earth in my vanity!"

He swore by his great name, "From now on, I will never do this again to those who live on the Earth, and I will set a sign in the sky, and this will be a pledge of good faith between me and them forever, so long as the sky is above the Earth. This a covenant by my command. When I have desired to take hold of them, by the hand of the watchers on the day of tribulation and pain, because of this, I will cause my punishment and my anger to cover them," said God, the Lord of Spirit. "You mighty kings who live on the Earth, see my chosen one, how he sits on the throne of glory and judges Azazel, and all his associates, and all his armies in the name of the Lord of Spirit."

Book of Parables - Chapter 20

I SAW THERE THE ARMIES of the punishing watchers leaving, and they held whips and chains of iron and bronze. I asked the peaceful watcher who went with me, "Who are these who hold the whips going to?"

He answered me, "To their chosen and beloved ones, that they may be thrown into the chasm of the abyss of the valley. Then that valley will be filled with their chosen and beloved, and the days of their lives will be at an end, and the days of their leading astray will not be considered again. In those days the watchers will return and hurl themselves in the east on the Persians and Medes.[P12] They will stir up the kings, so that a spirit of unrest will come on them, and they will rouse them from their thrones, that they may break out like lions from their lairs, and as hungry wolves among their flocks. They will go up and walk over the lands of his chosen ones, and the lands of his chosen ones will be like a threshing-floor and a highway before them. But the city of my righteous will stop their horses. They will begin to fight among themselves, and their right hand will be strong against themselves, and a man will not know his brother, nor a son his father or his mother until there is no counting of the corpses through their slaughter, and their punishment will not be in vain. In those days Sheol will open its jaws, and they will be swallowed up into it and their destruction will be at an end. Sheol will devour the sinners in the presence of the elect."

Book of Parables - Chapter 21

THEN I SAW ANOTHER army of chariots with men riding on them,[P13] and flying on the winds from the east and west to the south. The thunder of their chariots was heard, and when this turmoil took place the holy ones from the sky noted it, and the pillars of the Earth were moved from their place, and the sound of was heard from the one end of the sky to the other, in one day. They will all bow down and worship the Lord of Spirit.

This is the end of the second Parable.

Book of Parables - Chapter 22

I BEGAN TO SPEAK THE third Parable concerning the righteous and chosen.

Blessed are you, you righteous and chosen, for glory will be your fate. The righteous will be in the light of the sun, and the chosen in the light of eternal life. The days of their life will be unending, and the days of the holy without number. They will seek the light and find righteousness with the Lord of Spirit. There will be peace for the righteous in the name of the Eternal Lord.

After this it will be told to the holy in the sky that they should seek out the secrets of righteousness, the heritage of faith, for the Earth has become bright as the sun, and the darkness has passed. [P14] There will be a light that never ends, and no end of its days will ever come, because the darkness will have been destroyed already, and the light will be established before the Lord of Spirit and the light of uprightness will be established forever before the Lord of Spirit.

Book of Parables - Chapter 23

IN THOSE DAYS, MY EYES saw the secrets of the lightning, and of the lights, and the judgments they execute, and they light up as a blessing or a curse, as the Lord of Spirit chooses. There I saw the secrets of the thunder, and how when it echos above in the sky and the sound is heard, and he caused me to see the judgments executed on the Earth, whether they are as good blessings, or as a curse, according to the word of the Lord of Spirit. After that all the secrets of the lights and lightning were shown to me, and they light up as blessing and satisfaction.

Book of Parables - Chapter 24

IN THE YEAR FIVE HUNDRED, in the seventh month, on the fourteenth day of the month in the life of Enoch.[P15]

In that Parable, I saw how a mighty quaking made the sky above the sky to quake, and the army of the Highest, and the watchers, a thousand thousands and ten thousand times ten thousand, were disturbed with a great disturbance. The Head of Days sat on the throne of his glory, and the watchers and the righteous stood around him.

A great trembling seized me, and fear took hold of me, and my loins gave way, and my reins dissolved, and I fell on my face. Michael sent another watcher from among the holy ones and he lifted me up, and once he had raised me my spirit returned, for I had not been able to endure the sight of this army, and the commotion and the quaking of the sky.

Michael asked me, "Why are you disturbed by such a vision? Until today have been the days of his mercy, and he has been merciful and patient towards those who live on the Earth. When the day, and the power, and the punishment, and the judgment come, which the Lord of Spirit has prepared for those who don't worship the righteous law, and for those who deny the righteous judgment, and for those who take his name in vain, that day is decided, for the chosen the covenant, but for sinners an inquisition. When the punishment of the Lord of Spirit will come on them, it will not be that the punishment of the Lord of Spirit will come in vain. It will slay the children with their mothers and the children with their fathers. Afterward, the judgment will take place according to his mercy and his patience."

On that day, two monsters were parted, a female monster named Leviathan, to live in the abysses of the seas above the fountains of the waters, and a male named Behemoth, who occupied with his beasts a wasteland named Dudael,[P16] on the east of the garden where the elect and righteous live, where my grandfather was taken up, the seventh from Adam,[P17] the first man whom the Lord of Spirit created. I asked the other watcher to show me the might of those monsters, how they were parted on one day and thrown, the one into the abysses of the sea, and the other to the dry land of the wilderness. He said to me, "'You, son of Adam, seek to know what is hidden."

[Enoch replied,] "The other watcher who went with me and showed me what was hidden told me what is first and last in the sky in the height, and beneath the Earth in the depth, and at the ends of the sky, and on the foundation of the sky. The other watcher who went with me and showed me what was hidden told me what is first and last in the sky in the height, and beneath the Earth in the depth, and at the ends of the sky, and on the foundation of the sky. The thunders according to the places where they fall, and all the divisions that are made among the lightning that may light up, and their army that will instantly obey. The thunder has places of rest assigned while it is waiting to sound, and the thunder and lightning are inseparable, and although they are not one, they both go together through the spirit and don't separate. When the lightning flashes, the thunder speaks its voice, and the spirit enforces a pause between the two and divides them equally. The treasury of their blasts is like the sand, and each one of them as it blasts is held in with a bridle, and turned back by the power of the spirit, and pushed forward according to the many quarters of the Earth."

[Enoch continued,] "The spirit of the sea is masculine and strong, and according to the might of his strength he draws it back with a rein, and in like manner it is driven forward and disperses amid all the mountains of the Earth. The spirit of the hoar-frost is his own watcher, and the spirit of the hail is a good watcher. The spirit of the snow has forgotten his chambers on account of his strength. There is a special spirit there, and that which ascends from it is like smoke and is named frost. The spirit of the mist is not united with them in their chambers, but it has a special chamber, for its course is glorious both in light and in darkness, and in winter and in summer, and in its chamber is a watcher. The spirit of the dew lives at the limits of the sky and is connected with the chambers of the rain, and its course is in winter and summer, and its clouds and the clouds of the mist are connected, and the one gives to the other. When the spirit of the rain goes out from its chamber, the watchers come and open the chamber and lead it out, and when it is diffused over the whole Earth it unites with the water on the Earth. Whensoever it unites with the water on the Earth [... missing text ...] The waters are for those who live on the Earth, for they are nourishment for the Earth from the Highest who is in the sky. Therefore there is a measure for the rain, and the watchers take it in turns. These things I saw towards the Garden of the Righteous."

The peaceful watcher who was with me said to me, "These two monsters, created properly by the greatness of God, will feed [... missing text ...][P18]

Book of Parables - Chapter 25

I SAW IN THOSE DAYS, how long cords were given to those watchers, and they took for themselves wings and flew, and they went towards the north. I asked the watcher, "Why have they taken these cords and flown away?"

He answered, "They have gone to measure."

The watcher who went with me said to me, "These will bring the measures of the righteous, and the ropes of the righteous to the righteous, that they may protect themselves in the name of the Lord of Spirit forever and ever. The chosen will begin to live with the chosen, and those are the measures which will be given to faith and which will strengthen righteousness. These measures will reveal all the secrets of the depths of the Earth, and those who have been destroyed by the desert, and those who have been devoured by the beasts, and those who have been devoured by the fish of the sea, and all who live above in the sky received a command and power and one voice and one light like to fire. As one they blessed and extolled and praised with wisdom, and they were wise in speech and the spirit of life."

"The Lord of Spirit placed the chosen one on the throne of glory. He will judge all the works of the holy above in the sky, and in the balance will their deeds be weighed. When he lifts his countenance to judge their secret ways according to the word of the name of the Lord of Spirit, and their path according to the way of the righteous judgment of the Lord of Spirit, then will they all with one voice speak and bless, and glorify and extol and sanctify the name of the Lord of Spirit."

"He will summon all the army of the skies and all the holy ones above, and the army of God, the cherubs,[P19] seraphs,[P20] and flying-wheels,[P21] and all the watchers of power, and all the watchers of principalities, and the chosen one, and the other powers on the Earth above the water. On that day, all will raise his voice, and bless and glorify and exalt in the spirit of faith, and in the spirit of wisdom, and the spirit of patience, and the spirit of mercy, and the spirit of judgment and peace, and in the spirit of goodness, and will all say with one voice, "Blessed is he, and may the name of the Lord of Spirit be blessed forever and ever."

All who don't sleep in the sky above will bless him. All the holy ones who are in the sky will bless him, and all the chosen who live in the garden of life. Every spirit of light who can bless, and glorify, and extol, and hallow your blessed name and all flesh will beyond measure glorify and bless your name forever and ever.

Great is the mercy of the Lord of Spirit, and he is patient, and all his works and all that he has created he has revealed to the righteous and elect in the name of the Lord of Spirit.

Book of Parables - Chapter 26

THE LORD COMMANDED the kings and the mighty and the exalted, and those who live on the Earth, saying, "Open your eyes and lift your horns[P22] if you can recognize the chosen one."

The Lord of Spirit seated him on the throne of his glory, and the spirit of righteousness was poured out on him, and the word of his mouth slays all the sinners, and all the unrighteous are destroyed from before his face. On that day, all the kings and the mighty will stand up and praise those who rule the Earth, and they will see and recognize how he sits on the throne of his glory, and righteousness is judged before him, and no lying words are spoken before him.

Pain comes on them then like on a woman in labor, and she has pain when giving birth when her child enters her vagina, and she has pain pushing it out. One group of them will look on the other, and they will be terrified, and they will be depressed in countenance, and pain will seize them when they see that son of Adam sitting on the throne of his glory. The kings and the mighty and all who possess the Earth will bless and glorify and extol him who rules over all, who was hidden. From the beginning, the son of Adam was hidden, and the Highest preserved him in the presence of his might and revealed him to the chosen. The congregation of the chosen and holy will be sown, and all the chosen will stand before him on that day.

All the kings, and the mighty, and the exalted, and those who rule the Earth, will all bow down before him on their faces, and worship and set their hope on that son of Adam, and petition him and supplicate for mercy at his hands. Nevertheless, that Lord of Spirit will press them so much that they will rush out from his presence, and their faces will be filled with shame, and the darkness will grow deeper on their faces. He will deliver them to the watchers for punishment, to execute vengeance on them because they have oppressed his children and his chosen, and they will be a spectacle for the righteous and his chosen. They will rejoice over them, because the anger of the Lord of Spirit rested on them, and his sword is drunk with their blood. The righteous and elect will be saved on that day, and they will never again see the face of the sinners and unrighteous. The Lord of Spirit will rule over them, and will they eat and lie down and rise up with that son of Adam forever and ever.

The righteous and chosen have risen from the Earth and ceased to be depressed. They have been clothed with garments of glory, and these will be the garments of life from the Lord of Spirit. Your garments will not grow old, or your glory passes away before the Lord of Spirit.

Book of Parables - Chapter 27

IN THOSE DAYS, WILL the mighty and the kings who possess the Earth, will beg to be granted them a little respite from his watchers of punishment to whom they were delivered, that they might bow down and worship before the Lord of Spirit, and confess their sins before him.

They will bless and praise the Lord of Spirit, saying, "Blessed is the Lord of Spirit, and Lord Moloch,[P40] and the Lord of the mighty, and the Lord of the rich, and the Lord of glory, and the Lord of wisdom, and splendid in every secret thing is in your power from generation to generation, and your glory forever and ever. Deep are all your secrets and innumerable, and your righteousness is beyond reckoning. We have learned that we should praise and bless Lord Moloch, he who is king over all kings."

They will say, "If only we had peace to praise and give thanks and confess our faith before his glory! We long for a little peace but cannot find it. We continue in difficulty but don't receive it. Light has vanished from before us, and darkness is our home forever and ever. We did not believe in him before or praise the name of the Lord of Spirit, or praise the Lord, but our faith was in the strength of our kingdom and our glory. In the day of our punishment and tribulation, he does not save us, and we find no peace for confessions that the Lord is true in all his works, in his judgments and his justice, and his judgments have no respect of persons. We pass away from before his face on account of our works, and all our sins are reckoned up in righteousness."

Then they will say to themselves, "Our minds are full of unrighteous gains, but it does not prevent us from descending into Sheol."

After that, their faces will be filled with darkness and shame before that son of Adam, and they will be driven from his presence, and the sword will remain between him and them.

Lord of Spirit said, "This is the ordinance and judgment concerning the mighty and the kings and the exalted and those who possess the Earth before the Lord of Spirit."

Book of Parables - Chapter 28

OTHER FORMS I SAW HIDDEN in that place. I heard the voice of the watcher saying, "These are the watchers who descended to the Earth, and revealed what was hidden to the children of men and seduced the children of men into sinning."

Book of Parables - Chapter 29

IN THOSE DAYS, NOAH saw the Earth, that it had sunk down and its destruction was near. He rose from there and went to the edge of the Earth, and cried out to his grandfather Enoch, and Noah said three times in an angry voice, "Hear me, hear me, hear me."

I, [Noah,] said to him, "Tell me what it is that is happening on the Earth, that the Earth is in such evil way and shaken, in case perhaps I perish with it."

On it, there was a great commotion, and across the Earth, a voice was heard from the sky, and I fell on my face. Enoch my grandfather came and stood by me, and asked, "Why have you cried to me with bitter crying and weeping? A command has gone out from the presence of the Lord concerning those who live on the Earth that their destruction in coming across the whole Earth because they have learned all the secrets of the watchers, and all the violence of the Satans, and all their powers, the most secret ones and all the power of those who practice sorcery, and the power of witchcraft, and the power of those who make molten images, and how silver is produced from the dust of the Earth, and how soft metal originates in the Earth. Lead and tin are not produced from the Earth in the beginning, it is a fountain that produces them, and a watcher stands there, and that watcher is preeminent."

After that my grandfather Enoch grabbed me by my hand and lifted me up, and said, "Go, for I have asked the Lord of Spirit regarding this commotion on the Earth, and he said to me, 'Because of their unrighteousness their judgment has been determined and will not be postponed by me forever. Because of the sorcery which they have studied and learned, the Earth and those who live on it will be destroyed.' These, they will have no respite forever, because they have shown them what was hidden, and they are the damned, but as for you, my son, the Lord of Spirit knows that you are pure, and guiltless of this sin concerning the secrets. He has fated your name to be among the holy, and will preserve you among those who live on the Earth, and has destined your righteous seed both for kingship and for great honors, and from your seed will proceed a fountain of the righteous and holy without number for ever."

Book of Parables - Chapter 30

AFTER THAT HE SHOWED me the watchers of punishment who are prepared to come and let loose all the powers of the waters which are beneath in the Earth to bring judgment and destruction on all who live on the Earth. The Lord of Spirit gave commandment to the watchers who were heading out, that they should not cause the waters to rise but should hold them in check, for those watchers were over the powers of the waters.

I left the presence of Enoch.

Book of Parables - Chapter 31

IN THOSE DAYS, THE word of God came to me and he said, "Noah, your fate has come up before me, a fate without blame, a fate of love and uprightness. Now the watchers are making a wooden [ark,] and when they have completed that task I will place my hand on it and preserve it, and there will come out from it the seed of life, and a change will set in so that the Earth will not remain without inhabitants. I will keep your descendants before me forever and ever, and I will spread abroad to those who live with you. It will not be unfruitful on the face of the Earth, but it will be blessed and multiply on the Earth in the name of the Lord."

He will imprison those watchers, who have been unrighteous in that burning valley which my grandfather Enoch had formerly shown me in the west among the mountains of gold and silver and iron and soft metal and tin. I saw that valley in which there was a great convulsion and a convulsion of the waters. When all this took place, from that fiery molten metal and from the convulsion of in that place, there was produced a smell of sulfur, and it was connected with those waters and that valley of the watchers who had led astray burned beneath that land. Through its valleys flowed streams of fire, where these watchers are punished who had led astray those who live on the Earth.

The waters will in those days serve the kings, and mighty, and exalted, and all those who live on the Earth. They will heal the body but punish the spirit. Now, their spirit is full of lust, and they will be punished in their body, for they have denied the Lord of Spirit, and see their punishment daily, and yet do not believe in his name. As the burning of their bodies becomes severe, in proportion a corresponding change will take place in their spirit forever and ever, as before the Lord of Spirit none will state an idle word. The judgment will come on them, because they believe in the lust of their body and deny the Lord of Spirit. Those same waters will change in those days, for when those watchers are punished in these waters, these water-springs will change their temperature, and when the watchers ascend, this water of the springs will change and become cold.

I heard Michael say, "This judgment where the watchers are judged is a testimony for the kings and the mighty who possess the Earth, because these waters of judgment minister to the healing of the body of the kings and the lust of their body, therefore they will not see and will not believe that those waters will change and become a fire which burns forever."

Book of Parables - Chapter 32

AFTER THAT MY GRANDFATHER Enoch gave me the teaching of all the secrets in the Book in the Parables which had been given to him, and he wrote them together for me in the words of the Book of the Parables.

On that day, Michael said to Raphael, "The power of the spirit makes me tremble because of the severity of the judgment of the secrets, and the judgment of the watchers. Who can endure the severe judgment which has been executed, and before which they melt away?"

Michael continued, and said to Raphael, "Who is he whose heart is not softened concerning it, and whose reins are not troubled by this word of judgment that has gone out on them because of those who have led them away?"

It happened when he stood before the Lord of Spirit, Michael said to Raphael, "I will not take their case before the eyes of the Lord, for the Lord of Spirit has been angry with them because they act as if they were the Lord. Therefore all that is hidden will cover them forever and ever, for neither watcher or man has his portion, but alone they have received their judgment forever and ever."

Book of Parables - Chapter 33

[MICHAEL CONTINUED,] "After this judgment, they will terrify and make those on the Earth tremble because they have been shown this."

See the names of those watchers, and these are their names: the first of them is Samyaza, the second Aristiqifa,[P23] and the third Armen,[P24] the fourth Kokabiel, the fifth Turael,[P25] the sixth Ramiel, the seventh Danel, the eighth Nuqael,[P26] the ninth Baraqiel, the tenth Azazel, the eleventh Armaros, the twelfth Batariel, the thirteenth Busaseial,[P27] the fourteenth Ananiel, the fifteenth Turel,[P28] and the sixteenth Simapesiel,[P29] the seventeenth Jetrel,[P30] the eighteenth Tumael,[P31] the nineteenth Turiel, the twentieth Rumael,[P32] the twenty-first Azazel.[P33] These are the chiefs of the watchers and their names, and their chief ones over hundreds and fifties and tens.

The name of the first was Yeqon.[P34] He was the one who led astray all the sons of God, and brought them down to the Earth, and led them astray through the daughters of men.

The second was named Asbeel.[P35] He gave the holy sons of God evil counsel and led them astray so that they defiled their bodies with the daughters of men.

The third was named Gadreel.[P36] He showed the children of men all the death-blows and led Eve astray. He taught the weapons of death to the sons of men: the shield, coat of armor, sword, and all the other weapons of death. Because of him, those who live on the Earth have fought from that day and forever.

The fourth was named Penemue.[P37] He taught the children of men the bitter and the sweet, and he taught them all the secrets of their wisdom. He instructed mankind in writing with ink and paper, and thereby many sinned from eternity to eternity and until this day. For men were not created for such a purpose, to confirm their good faith with pen and ink. For men were created exactly like the watchers, to the intent that they should continue pure and righteous, and death, which destroys everything, could not have taken hold of them, but through this their knowledge they are perishing, and through this power it is consuming me.

The fifth was named Kasdaye.[P38] He showed the children of men all the wicked ways of attacking spirits and demons, and how to kill the embryo in the womb so it would die, and how to kill with serpent's venom from the serpent called Tabaa'et which is caught in the noon-time heat.

This is the task of Kasbeel, the chief of the oath which he showed to the holy ones when he dwelt high above in glory, and its name is Biqa. He asked Michael to show him the hidden name, that he might enunciate it in the oath so that those might quake before that name and oath who revealed all that was in secret to the children of men. This is the power of this oath, for it is powerful and strong, and he placed this oath Akae in the hand of Michael. These are the secrets of this oath [...missing text...]

They are strong through his oath. The sky was suspended before the world was created, and forever.

Through it, the Earth was built on the water, and from the secret recesses in the mountains come beautiful waters, from the creation of the world and to eternity.

Through that oath, the sea was created, and as its foundation, he made the sand it to protect it when it became angry, and it did not dare pass beyond it from the creation of the world to eternity.

Through that oath are the depths made secure, and stay and don't stir from their place from eternity to eternity. Through that oath, the sun and moon complete their course and don't deviate not from their course from eternity to eternity. Through that oath, the stars complete their course, and he called them by their names, and they answered him from eternity to eternity. In like manner, the spirits of the water, and the winds, and all zephyrs, follow paths from all the quarters of the winds.

There are the preserved voices of the thunder and the light of the lightning, and the preserved the chambers of the hail and the chambers of the hoarfrost, and the chambers of the mist, and the chambers of the rain and the dew. All these believe and give thanks before the Lord of Spirit, and praise with all their power and their food is the very act of thanksgiving. They thank and glorify and extol the name of the Lord of Spirit forever and ever.

This oath is strong in them and through it, they are kept in their paths and are preserved, and their course is not altered.

There was great joy among them, and they blessed and glorified and praised because the name of that son of Adam had been revealed to them. He sat on the throne of his glory, and the sum of judgment was given to the son of Adam, and he caused the sinners to die and be destroyed from off the face of the Earth, with those who have led the world astray. With chains will they be bound, and in their assemblage-place of destruction will they be imprisoned, and all their works vanish from the face of the Earth. From now on there will be nothing corruptible. For that son of Adam has appeared, and has seated himself on the throne of his glory, and all evil will pass away before his face, and the word of that son of Adam will go out and be strong before the Lord of Spirit.

This is the Third Parable of Enoch.

Book of Parables - Chapter 34

AFTER THIS, HE WAS taken up while still alive to that son of Adam and to the Lord of Spirit from among those who live on the Earth. He was taken up on the chariots of the spirit and his name vanished among them.

From that day I was no longer counted among them, and he set me between the two winds, between the North and the West, where the watchers took the cords to measure for me the place for the chosen and righteous. There I saw the first fathers and the righteous who from the beginning live in that place.

Book of Parables - Chapter 35

AFTER THIS, MY SPIRIT was changed and it ascended into the skies. I saw the holy sons of God. They were moving on flames of fire. Their garments were white and their clothing, and their faces shone like snow. I saw two streams of fire, and the light of that fire shone like hyacinth, and I fell on my face before the Lord of Spirit.

The watcher Michael one of the high-watchers seized me by my right hand, and lifted me up and led me out into all the secrets, and he showed me all the secrets of righteousness. He showed me all the secrets of the limits of the sky, and all the chambers of all the stars,[P39] and all the luminaries, and where they pass before the faces of the holy ones.

He moved my spirit into the sky above the sky, and I saw there a structure built of crystals, and between those crystals tongues of living fire. My spirit saw the wall which surrounded that house of fire, and on its four sides were streams full of living fire, and they surrounded that house. Around it were seraphs, cherubs, and flying-wheels. These are those who don't sleep and guard the throne of his glory.

I saw watchers who could not be counted, a thousand thousand, and ten thousand times ten thousand, circling that palace. Michael, Raphael, Gabriel, Penuel, and the holy watchers who are above the skies, went in and out of that palace. They came out from that palace, Michael, Gabriel, Raphael, Penuel, and many holy watchers without number. With them was the Head of Days, his hair white and pure as wool, and his clothing indescribable. I fell on my face, and my whole body became relaxed, and my spirit was transfigured.

Blessings went out of my mouth were pleasing before that Head of Days. That Head of Days came with Michael, Gabriel, Raphael, Penuel, and thousands and ten thousands of watchers without number.

He came to me and greeted me with his voice, saying, "This is the son of Adam who is born to righteousness. Righteousness lives in him, and he does not abandon following the Head of Days."

He said to me, "He proclaims to you peace in the name of the world to come. From here peace has proceeded since the creation of the world, and so it will be for you forever and ever. All will walk in his ways righteously and never forgot him. They will live with him, and their descendants and they will not be separated from him forever and ever. There will be the length of days with that son of Adam, and the righteous have peace and an upright path in the name of the Lord of Spirit forever and ever."

Astronomical Book - Chapter 1

THE BOOK OF THE COURSES of the luminaries of the sky, the relations of each, according to their classes, their dominion and their seasons, including their names and places of origin, and their months, which Uriel, the holy watcher, who was with me, who is their guide, showed me. He showed me all their laws exactly as they are, and how it will be for all the years of the world to eternity until the new creation is finished which lasts for eternity.

This is the first law of the luminaries: the sun rises in the eastern portals of the sky, and it sets in the western portals of the sky. I saw six portals in which the sun rises, and six portals in which the sun sets and the moon rises and sets in these portals, and the leaders of the stars and those who they lead: six in the east and six in the west, and all following each other accurately in their order. Also, there were many windows to the right and left of these portals.

First, the great luminary comes out, named Shemesh,[A1] and his circumference is like the circumference of the sky, and he is filled with light and heating fire. He rides a chariot and is driven by the wind. The sun goes down from the sky and returns through the north to reach the east, and is so guided that he comes to the appropriate portal and shines in the face of the sky. In this way, he rises in the first month in the great portal, which is the fourth of the six portals in the east. In that fourth portal from which the sun rises in the first month are twelve window-openings, from which come a flame when they are opened in their season. When the sun rises in the sky, he comes out through that fourth portal thirty mornings in a row and sets accurately in the fourth portal in the west of the sky. During this period the day becomes daily longer and the night nightly shorter until the thirtieth morning. On that day the day is longer than the night by a ninth part, and the day amounts exactly to ten parts and the night to eight parts.

The sun rises from that fourth portal, and sets in the fourth and returns to the fifth portal of the east thirty mornings, and rises from it and sets in the fifth portal. Then the day becomes longer by two parts and amounts to eleven parts, and the night becomes shorter and amounts to seven parts. It returns to the east and enters into the sixth portal, and rises and sets in the sixth portal one-and-thirty mornings on account of its sign. On that day, the day becomes longer than the night, and the day becomes double the night, and the day becomes twelve parts, and the night is shortened and becomes six parts.

The sun flies up to make the day shorter and the night longer, and the sun returns to the east and enters into the sixth portal, and rises from it and sets thirty mornings. When thirty mornings are accomplished, the day decreases by exactly one part and becomes eleven parts, and the night seven. The sun comes out from that sixth portal in the west, and goes to the east and rises in the fifth portal for thirty mornings, and sets in the west again in the fifth western portal. On that day, the day decreases by two parts and amounts to ten parts and the night to eight parts.

The sun comes out from that fifth portal and sets in the fifth portal of the west, and rises in the fourth portal for one-and-thirty mornings on account of its sign, and sets in the west. On that day, the day is equalized with the night and becomes of equal length, and the night amounts to nine parts and the day to nine parts.

The sun rises from that portal and sets in the west, and returns to the east and rises thirty mornings in the third portal and sets in the west in the third portal. On that day the night becomes longer than the day, and night becomes longer than night, and day shorter than day till the thirtieth morning, and the night amounts exactly to ten parts and the day to eight parts.

The sun rises from that third portal and sets in the third portal in the west and returns to the east, and for thirty mornings rises in the second portal in the east, and in like manner sets in the second portal in the west of the sky. On that day the night amounts to eleven parts and the day to seven parts. The sun rises on that day from that second portal and sets in the west in the second portal and returns to the east into the first portal for one-and-thirty mornings, and sets in the first portal in the west of the sky.

On that day, the night becomes longer and amounts to the double of the day: and the night amounts exactly to twelve parts and the day to six. The sun has traversed the divisions of his orbit and turns again on those divisions of his orbit, and enters that portal thirty mornings and sets also in the west opposite to it. On that night, has the night decreased in length by a ninth part, and the night has become eleven parts and the day seven parts.

The sun has returned and entered into the second portal in the east, and returns on those divisions of his orbit for thirty mornings, rising and setting. On that day the night decreases in length, and the night amounts to ten parts and the day to eight. On that day, the sun rises from that portal, and sets in the west, and returns to the east, and rises in the third portal for one-and-thirty mornings, and sets in the west of the sky. On that day, the night decreases and amounts to nine parts, and the day to nine parts and the night is equal to the day and the year is exactly as to its days three hundred and sixty-four.

The length of the day and of the night, and the shortness of the day and of the night rise, through the course of the sun these distinctions are made. So it comes that its course becomes daily longer, and its course nightly shorter. This is the law and the course of the sun, and his return as often as he returns sixty times and rises, the great luminary which is named the Sun, forever and ever. He who rises is the great luminary and is so named according to its appearance, as the Lord[A2] commanded. As he rises, so he sets and does not stop or rest, but runs day and night, and his light is seven times brighter than that of the moon, but as regards size they are both equal.

Astronomical Book - Chapter 2

AFTER THIS LAW, I SAW another law dealing with the lesser luminary, which is named the Yarikh.[A3] Her circumference is like the circumference of the sky, and her chariot in which she rides is driven by the wind, and light is given to her in proportion. Her rising and setting change every month. Her days are like the days of the sun, and when her light is full it is one-seventh a bright as the light of the sun. When she rises, her first phase, she comes out in the east on the thirtieth morning, and on that day she becomes visible and shows as the first phase of the moon on the thirtieth day, together with the sun in the portal where the sun rises. One half of her comes out on the seventh day, and her whole circumference is dark, except one-seventh part of it, shining the fourteenth part of her light. When she receives one-seventh part of the half of her light, her light amounts to one-seventh and a half part of it.

She sets with the sun, and when the sun rises the moon rises with him and receives the half of one part of the light, and in that night in the beginning of her morning the moon sets with the sun and is invisible that night with the fourteen parts and the half of one of them. She rises on that day with exactly a seventh part, and comes out and withdraws from the rising of the sun, and in her remaining days, she brightens across the other thirteen parts.

Astronomical Book - Chapter 3

I SAW ANOTHER PATH, a law for her: how according to that law she performs her monthly revolution.

All these Uriel, the holy watcher who is the leader of them all, showed to me, and their positions and I wrote down their positions as he showed them to me, and I wrote down their months as they were, and the appearance of their lights until the end of fifteen. On the first day she shines all her light in the east, and on the last day is dark in the west.

In certain months she alters her settings, and in certain months she pursues her own peculiar course. In two months the moon sets with the sun, in those two middle portals the third and the fourth. She comes out for seven days, and turns about and returns again through the portal where the sun rises, and shines all her light, and she withdraws from the sun, and in eight days enters the sixth portal from which the sun comes out. When the sun comes out from the fourth portal she comes out for a week until she comes out from the fifth and turns back again in a week into the fourth portal and shines all her light, and she withdraws and enters into the first portal for eight days. She returns again for seven days into the fourth portal from which the sun comes out.

I saw their position, and how the moon rose and the sunset in those days. If five years are added together the sun has an extra thirty days, and all the days which accrue to it for one of those five years, when they are full, amount to 364 days. The extra of the sun and of the stars amounts to six days. Six days every year for five years adds up to 30 days. The moon falls behind the sun and stars 30 days. The sun and the stars bring in all the years exactly, so that they do not advance or delay their position by a single day for eternity, but complete the years with perfect justice in 364 days. In three years there are 1092 days, and in five years 1820 days, so that in eight years there are 2912 days.

For the moon, the days add up in three years to 1062 days, and in five years she falls 50 days behind. In five years there are 1770 days so that for the moon the days in eight years amount to 2832 days. So in eight years, she falls behind 80 days. In total, she falls behind 80 days in 8 years.

The year is accurately completed consistently, with their world-stations and the stations of the sun, which rise through the portals that it rises and sets for 30 days.

Astronomical Book - Chapter 4

THE LEADERS OF THE heads of the thousands, who are placed over all of creation and all the stars, also have to do with the four intercalary days, being inseparable from their office, according to the reckoning of the year, and these render service on the four days which are not considered in the reckoning of the year. Owing to them, men make mistakes during them, for those luminaries render service on the world-stations, one in the first portal, one in the third portal of the sky, one in the fourth portal, and one in the sixth portal, and the exactness of the year is accomplished through its separate three hundred and sixty-four stations.

The watcher Uriel showed to me the signs, and the times, and the years and the days. The Lord of Glory[A13] has set Uriel forever over all the luminaries of the sky, in the sky and the world, that they should rule over the face of the sky, and are seen on the Earth, and be leaders for the day and the night, and all the ministering creatures which make their revolution in all the chariots of the sky.

Similarly, Uriel showed me twelve doors, open in the circumference of the sun's chariot in the sky, through which the rays of the sun break out, and warmth is diffused across the Earth from them when they are opened at their appointed seasons. When they are opened and stand open in the limits of the sky, the winds and the spirit of the dew come out. As for the twelve portals in the sky, at the edge of the Earth, from which the sun, moon, stars, and all the creations of the sky, come out in the east and enter in the west. There are many windows open to the left and right of them, and one window in its season produces warmth, corresponding to those doors from which the stars come out as he has commanded them, and in which they set corresponding to their number.

I saw flying-chariots in the sky,[A4] crossing the world above those portals through which revolve the stars that never set. One is larger than all the rest, and it is that which makes its path across the entire world.

Astronomical Book - Chapter 5

AT THE EDGE OF THE Earth, I saw twelve portals open to all the quarters from which the winds come out and blow over the Earth. Three of them open on the face of the skies, and three in the west, and three on the right of the sky, and three on the left. The first three are those are in the east, and three are in the north, and three of those are to the left of the south, and three to the west. Through four of these come winds of blessing and prosperity, and from those eight come hurtful wind, and when they are sent out, they bring destruction across all the Earth and on the water on it, and on all those who live on it, and everything in the water and on the land. The first wind from those portals, called the east wind, comes out through the first portal which is in the east, heading towards the south. It brings desolation, drought, heat, and destruction. Through the second portal in the middle comes that which is fitting, rain, fruitfulness, prosperity, and dew. Through the third portal which lies toward the north comes cold and drought.

After these come out the south winds through three portals. Through the first portal to the east comes out a hot wind. Through the middle portal next to it, fragrant smells, dew, rain, prosperity, and health come out. Through the third portal lying to the west comes out dew and rain, locusts and desolation.

After these, the north winds from the seventh portal in the east come dew and rain, locusts and desolation. From the middle portal health, rain, dew, and prosperity come. Through the third portal in the west come clouds and hoar-frost, and snow and rain, and dew and locusts.

After these four, are the west winds. Through the first portal in the north comes out dew, hoar-frost, cold, snow, and frost. From the middle portal comes out dew, rain, prosperity, and blessing. Through the last portal in the south comes out drought, desolation, burning, and destruction.

The twelve portals of the four quarters of the sky are therefore explained, and all their laws and all their plagues and all their benefactions have I showed to you, my son Methuselah.[A5]

Astronomical Book - Chapter 6

THE FIRST QUARTER IS called the east because it is the first. The second, the south, because of the Highest[A6] will descend there, yes, in quite a special sense he who is blessed forever will descend. The west quarter is named 'diminished' because there all the luminaries of the sky wane and go down. The fourth quarter, named the north, is divided into three parts. The first of them is for men to live in. The second contains seas of water, abysses, forests, rivers, darkness, and clouds. The third part contains the garden of righteousness.

I saw seven high mountains, higher than all the mountains which are on the Earth, and from there comes hoar-frost, and days, seasons, and years pass away. I saw seven rivers on the earth larger than all other rivers. One of them coming from the west pours its waters into the Great Sea.[A7] These two come from the north to the sea and pour their waters into the Erythraean Sea[A8] in the east. The remaining four drain out on the side of the north to their own sea, two of them to the Erythraean Sea, and two into the Great Sea and discharge themselves there and according to some into the desert. Seven great islands I saw in the sea and on the mainland, two on the mainland and five in the Great Sea.

Astronomical Book - Chapter 7

THE FOLLOWING ARE THE names of the sun: the first is Orjares and the second is Tomas.[A9] The moon has four names: the first name is Asonja, the second Ebla, the third Benase, and the fourth Erae.[A10] These are the two great luminaries. Their circumference is like the circumference of the sky, and the size of the circumference of both is the same. Within the circumference of the sun, there is seven times the light as the moon, and in specific measures, it is transferred until the seventh portion of the sun is exhausted.

They set and enter the portals of the west, and make their revolution by the north, and come out through the eastern portals on the face of the sky. When the moon rises one-fourteenth part appears in the sky, the light becomes full in her, on the fourteenth day she shines her light. Fifteen parts of light are transferred to her until the fifteenth day when her light is accomplished, according to the sign of the year, and she becomes fifteen parts, and the moon grows by fourteenth parts. In her waning, she decreases on the first day to fourteen parts of her light, on the second to thirteen parts of light, on the third to twelve, on the fourth to eleven, on the fifth to ten, on the sixth to nine, on the seventh to eight, on the eighth to seven, on the ninth to six, on the tenth to five, on the eleventh to four, on the twelfth to three, on the thirteenth to two, on the fourteenth to the half of a seventh, and all her remaining light disappears wholly on the fifteenth. In certain months, the month has twenty-nine days and once twenty-eight.

Uriel showed me another law. When light is transferred to the moon, and on which side it is transferred to her by the sun. During all the time during which the moon is growing brighter, she is transferring it to herself when opposite to the sun during fourteen days, and when she is illumined throughout, her light is full in the sky. On the first day, she is called the new moon, for on that day the light rises on her. She becomes full moon exactly on the day when the sun sets in the west, and from the east, she rises at night, and the moon shines the whole night through until the sun rises over against her and the moon is seen over against the sun. On the side from where the light of the moon comes forth, there again she wanes until all the light vanishes and all the days of the month are at an end, and her circumference is empty, void of light. Three months she makes of thirty days, and at her time she makes three months of twenty-nine days each, in which she accomplishes her waning in the first period of time, and the first portal for one hundred and seventy-seven days. In the time of her leaving she appears for three months of thirty days each, and for three months she appears in twenty-nine days. At night, she looks like a man for twenty days each time, and by day she appears in the sky, and there is nothing in her except her light.

Astronomical Book - Chapter 8

NOW, MY SON, I HAVE shown you everything, and the law of all the stars of the sky is completed. He showed me all the laws of these for every day, and for every season of bearing rule, and for every year, and for its going out, and for the order prescribed to it every month and every week: The waning of the moon which takes place in the sixth portal, for in this sixth portal her light is accomplished, and after that, there is the beginning of the waning. The waning which takes place in the first portal in its season, until one hundred and seventy-seven days are accomplished, calculated as twenty-five weeks and two days. She falls behind the sun and the order of the stars exactly five days in the course of one period, and when this place which you see has been traversed. Such is the picture and sketch of every luminary which Uriel the archangel, who is their leader, showed to me.

Astronomical Book - Chapter 9

IN THOSE DAYS, THE watcher Uriel said to me, "Look, I have shown you everything, Enoch, and I have revealed everything to you, so you can understand the sun and the moon, and the leaders of the stars of the sky and all those who turn them, their tasks and times and departures. In the days of the sinners, the years will be shortened, and their descendants will be slow on their lands and fields, and all things on the Earth will alter, and will not appear in their time. The rain will be kept back. The sky will withhold it."

"In those times the fruits of the Earth will be reversed, and will not grow in their time, and the fruits of the trees will be held back in their time. The moon will change her order, and not appear at her time. In those days the sun will be seen and he will journey in the evening on the extremity of the great chariot in the west and will shine more brightly than normal. Many chiefs of the stars will transgress the order. These will alter their orbits and tasks, and not appear at the seasons prescribed to them. The whole order of the stars will be concealed from the sinners, and the thoughts of those on the Earth will error concerning them, and they will be altered from all their ways, they will error and think of them as gods. Evil will be multiplied in them, and punishment will come on them to destroy all."

Astronomical Book - Chapter 10

HE SAID TO ME, "ENOCH, see these heavenly tablets, and read what is written on them, and copy everything."

I saw the heavenly tablets, and read everything which was written and understood everything, and read the book of all the deeds of mankind, and of all the children of flesh that will be on the Earth to the remotest generations. Immediately, I blessed the great Lord Moloch[A12] in glory forever, in that he has made all the works of the world and I praised the Lord because of his patience and blessed him because of the children of men.

Then I said, "The man who dies in righteousness and goodness is blessed, as there is no book of unrighteousness written about him, and nothing will be found against him on the day of judgment."

Those seven holy ones brought me and placed me on the Earth before the door of my house, and said to me, "Tell everything to your son Methuselah, and show to all your children that no flesh is righteous in the sight of the Lord, for he is their creator. We will leave you with your son for one year, until you give your commands, that you may teach your children and record it for them, and testify to all your children. In the second year, we will take you from among them. Let your heart be strong, for the good will announce righteousness to the good. The righteous with the righteous will rejoice and will offer congratulation to one another. But, the sinners will die with the sinners, and the apostate goes down with the apostate. Those who practice righteousness will die on account of the deeds of men, and be taken away on account of the doings of the godless."

Then they stopped speaking to me, and I returned to my people, blessing the Lord of the world.

Astronomical Book - Chapter 11

NOW, MY SON METHUSELAH, all these things I am retelling you and writing down for you, and I have revealed to you everything, and given you books concerning all these, my son Methuselah, so preserve the books from your father's hand, and give them to future generations of the world.

I have given wisdom to you and your children, and the descendants that will come from you, that they may give it to their children for future generations, so this wisdom passes into their thoughts. Those who understand it will not sleep but will listen with their ears that they may learn this wisdom, and it will please those that eat better than good food.

Blessed are all the righteous, blessed are all those who walk in the way of righteousness and don't sin like the sinners, in considering all their days in which the sun crosses the sky, entering into and departing from the portals for thirty days with the heads of thousands of the order of the stars, together with the four which are calculated and divide the four portions of the year, which lead them and enter with them four days. Because of them, men will be at fault and not considering them in the whole calculation of the year. Yes, men will be at fault, and not recognize them accurately. They belong to the calculation of the year and are recorded correctly forever, one in the first portal and one in the third, and one in the fourth and one in the sixth, and the year is completed in three hundred and sixty-four days.

The account of it is accurate and the recorded reckoning of exact. The luminaries and months and festivals, and years and days, has Uriel showed and revealed to me, to whom the Lord of the whole creation of the world has subjected the host of the sky. He has power overnight and day in the sky to cause the light to give light to men. Sun, moon, and stars, and all the powers of the sky which revolve in their circular chariots. These are the orders of the stars, which set in their places, and their seasons and festivals and months.

These are the names of those who lead them, who watch that they enter at their times, in their orders, in their seasons, in their months, in their periods of dominion, and their positions. Their four leaders who divide the four parts of the year enter first, and after them the twelve leaders of the orders who divide the months, and for the three hundred and sixty days there are heads over thousands who divide the days, and for the four intercalary days there are the leaders which sunder the four parts of the year.

These heads over thousands are intercalated between leader and leader, each behind a station, but their leaders divide them. These are the names of the leaders who divide the four parts of the year which are ordained: Milki-El,[A11] Hel'emmelek, Mel'ejal, and Narel. The names of those who lead them, Adnar'el, Ijasusa'el, and 'Elome'el. These three follow the leaders of the orders, and there is one that follows the three leaders of the orders which follow those leaders of stations that divide the four parts of the year.

At the beginning of the year Melkejal rises first and rules, who is named Tam'aini and sun, and all the days of his dominion while he bears rule are ninety-one days. These are the signs of the days which are to be seen on Earth in the days of his dominion: sweat, and heat, and calms; and all the trees carry fruit, and leaves are produced on all the trees, and the harvest of wheat, and the rose-flowers, and all the flowers which come forth in the field, but the trees of the winter season become withered. These are the names of the leaders who are under them: Berka'el, Zelebs'el, and another who is added as head of a thousand, called Hilujaseph, and the days of the dominion of this are at an end.

The next leader after him is Hel'emmelek, whom one names the shining sun, and all the days of his light are ninety-one days. These are the signs of his days on the Earth, glowing heat and dryness, and the trees ripen their fruits and produce all their fruits ripe and ready, and the sheep pair and become pregnant, and all the fruits of the Earth are gathered in, and everything that is in the fields, and the wine-press: these things take place in the days of his dominion. These are the names, and the orders, and the leaders of those heads of thousands: Gida'ijal, Ke'el, and He'el, and the name of the head of a thousand which is added to them, Asfa'el', and the days of his dominion are at an end.

Dream Visions - Chapter 1

———

[ENOCH SAID,] MY SON Methuselah, I will tell you all the visions that I have seen, and retell them to you."

I had two visions before I took a wife, and they were quite different from each other. The first, was when I was learning to write, and the second was before I took your mother. They were nightmares. I prayed to the Lord^{D1} about them.

I had laid down in the house of my grandfather Mahalalel when I had a dream of the sky collapsing, and falling on the Earth. When it fell to the Earth I saw how the Earth was swallowed up in a great abyss,^{D2} and mountains collapsed onto mountains, and hills sank down into hills, and high trees were ripped from their roots and hurled down and sunk into the abyss. When I saw it, words came to my mouth, and I shouted loudly, "The Earth is destroyed."

My grandfather Mahalalel woke me, as I lay near him, and asked, "Why are you crying, my son? Why are you making so much noise?"

I told him my dream, and he said, "A terrible thing have you seen, my son. Your dream-vision is about a terrible time because of the secret sins of the Earth. It must sink into the abyss and be destroyed with great destruction. Now, my son, rise and pray to the Lord of Glory,^{D9} since you are a believer, that a remnant may remain on the Earth, and that he may not destroy the whole Earth. My son, from the sky all this will come on the Earth, and on the Earth, there will be great destruction."

After that, I rose and prayed. I begged and begged, and wrote down my prayer for all the generations of the world, and I will show everything to you, my son Methuselah. When I had gone out below and seen the sky, and the sun rising in the east, and the moon setting in the west, and a few stars, and the whole Earth, and everything as he had known it in the beginning, then I blessed the Lord of judgment and praised him because he had made the sun to come out from the portals of the east, and he ascended and rose in the face of the sky, and set out and kept traveling his path.

Dream Visions - Chapter 2

———

I LIFTED MY HANDS IN righteousness and blessed the holy and great one, and spoke with the breath of my mouth, and with the tongue of flesh, which God has made for the children of men, that they should speak with when he gave them breath and a tongue and a mouth that they should speak with, saying, "Blessed are you, lord Moloch,[D3] great and mighty in your greatness, Lord of all creation of the sky, king of kings and god of the whole world. Your power and kingship and greatness abide forever and ever and throughout all generations your dominion. All the skies are your throne forever, and the whole Earth is your footstool forever and ever.

You made and rule all things, and nothing is too difficult for you, wisdom does not depart from the place of your throne, or turns away from your presence. You know and see and hear everything, and there is nothing hidden from you, for you see everything. Now the watchers[D4] from the skies are guilty of trespassing, and against the flesh of men, your anger is until the great day of judgment. Now, God and Lord and Great Moloch, I beg and plead with you to fulfill my prayer, and leave me descendants on Earth, and not destroy all the flesh of men, and make the Earth uninhabited, so there should be eternal destruction. Now, my lord, destroy from the Earth the flesh which has aroused your anger, but the flesh of righteousness and uprightness establish as a plant of the eternal seed, and don't hide your face from the prayer of your servant, my lord."

Dream Visions - Chapter 3

[ENOCH SAID,] "AFTER this I had another dream, and I will tell you the whole dream, my son."

Enoch rose and said to his son Methuselah, "I will speak to you my son, hear my words. Listen to the dream-vision of your father. Before I married your mother Edna, I had a dream in my bed. I saw a bull come out from the Earth, and that bull was white. After it came out a heifer, and along with her came out two bulls, one of them black and the other red. That black bull gored the red one and chased him across the Earth, and I could no longer see the red bull on Earth. That black bull grew and the heifer mated with him, and I saw many oxen proceeded from him which resembled and followed him. That cow, that first one, left the presence of that first bull in order to seek the red one, but did not find him, and mourned in great sadness over him and wanted him. I looked until that first bull came to her and silenced her, and from that time onward she cried no more. After that she carried another white bull, and after him she carried many bulls and black cows."

"I saw in my sleep that white bull likewise grew and become a great white bull, and from him came many white bulls, and they resembled him. They began to father many white bulls, which resembled them, many one following the other."

Dream Visions - Chapter 4

———

"I SAW AGAIN WITH MY eyes as I slept. I looked at the sky above, and saw a star fall from the sky, and it rose and ate and pastured among those oxen. After that I saw the large black oxen, and saw they all changed their stalls and pastures and their livestock, and began to live with each other. Again I saw in the dream, as I looked towards the sky, and I saw many stars descend and fall from the sky following that first star, and they became bulls among those livestock and pastured with them and among them. I looked at them and saw, and look they all let out their gentiles, like horses, and began to mount the cows of the oxen, and they all became pregnant and carried elephants, camels, and donkeys. All the oxen were afraid them and were scared of them, and began to bite with their teeth and devour, and gore with their horns. They began to devour those oxen, and look all the children of the Earth began to tremble and quake before them and to flee from them."

Dream Visions - Chapter 5

"I SAW HOW THEY BEGAN to gore each other and to devour each other, and the Earth began to cry aloud. I raised my eyes again to the sky, and I saw in the vision, and look there came from the sky beings who were like white men, and four went out from that place and three with them. Those three that had come out last grasped me by my hand and took me up, away from the generations of the Earth, and raised me up to a lofty place, and showed me a tower raised high above the Earth,[D5] and all the hills were lower than it. One said to me, 'Stay here until you see everything that happens those elephants, camels, and donkeys, and the stars and the oxen, and all of them.'"

Dream Visions - Chapter 6

"I SAW ONE OF THOSE four who had come out first, and he seized that first star which had fallen from the sky, and bound it hand and foot and threw it into an abyss. Now, that abyss was narrow and deep, and horrible and dark. One of them drew a sword, and gave it to those elephants and camels and donkeys, and they began to kill each other, and the whole Earth quaked because of them. As I saw in the dream, and one of those four who had come out stoned them from the sky, and gathered and took all the great stars whose genitals were like those of horses, and tied them all up by their hands and feet, and through them in an abyss in the Earth."

Dream Visions - Chapter 7

———

"ONE OF THOSE FOUR WENT to that white bull and instructed him in a secret, without his being terrified. Even though he was born a bull, he became a man, and built for himself a great vessel and lived in it, and three bulls lived with him in that vessel, and they were covered within it. I raised my eyes towards the sky again and saw a high ceiling, with seven water torrents in it, and those torrents flowed great floods into a reservoir."

"I looked again and saw fountains opened on the surface of that great reservoir, and the water began to full up and rise to the surface, and I watched that reservoir until all its surface was covered with water. The water, the darkness, and mist increased on it, and as I observed the height of that water, that water rose above the height of the reservoir, and was streaming over the edge of the reservoir, and it fell on the Earth. All the livestock crowded together until I saw how they sank and were swallowed up and drowned in that water. But that vessel floated on the water, while all the oxen and elephants and camels and donkeys sank to the bottom with all the animals, so that I could no longer see them, and they were not able to escape but drowned and sank into the depths."

"I continued to dream until those water torrents were removed from that high ceiling, and the chasms of the Earth were filled in and other abysses were opened. Then the water began to run down into these, until the Earth became visible, and that vessel settled on the Earth, and the darkness left and light appeared. That white bull which had become a man came out of that vessel, and the three bulls with him, and one of those three was white like that bull, and one of them was red as blood, and one black, and that white bull departed from them."

"They began to bring out the domesticated animals and birds, so that there arose different kinds: lions, tigers, wolves, dogs, hyenas, wild boars, foxes, squirrels, hogs, falcons, vultures, kites, eagles, and ravens, and among them was born a white bull. They began to bite one another, but that white bull which was born among them fathered a wild donkey and a white bull along with them. The wild donkeys multiplied, but that bull which was born from him fathered a black wild boar and a white sheep, and the former fathered many boars, but that sheep fathered twelve sheep. When those twelve sheep had grown, they gave up one of them to the donkeys, and those donkeys again gave up that sheep to the wolves, and that sheep grew up among the wolves."

"The Lord brought the eleven sheep to live with it and to pasture with it among the wolves, and they multiplied and became many flocks of sheep. The wolves began to fear them, and they oppressed them until they destroyed their little ones, and they threw their young into a river of great water, but those sheep began to cry out loud on account of their little ones, and to complain to their Lord. A sheep which had been saved from the wolves fled and escaped to the wild donkeys, and I saw the sheep how they lamented and cried, and begged their Lord with all their might, until that Lord of the sheep descended to the voices of the sheep from a lofty home, and came to them and fed them."

"He called that sheep which had escaped the wolves, and spoke with it concerning the wolves that it should admonish them not to touch the sheep. The sheep went to the wolves obeying to the commands of the Lord, and another sheep met it and went with it, and the two went and entered together into the assembly of those wolves, and spoke with them and admonished them to not touch the sheep from from then on. On hearing it, I saw the wolves and how they oppressed the sheep greatly with all their power, and the sheep cried aloud."

"The Lord came to the sheep and they began to kill the wolves, and the wolves began to cry but the sheep became quiet and immediately stopped crying out. I watched the sheep until they departed from among the wolves, but the eyes of the wolves were blinded, and those wolves departed in pursuit of the sheep with all their power. The Lord of the sheep went with them as their leader, and all his sheep followed him, and his face was dazzling and glorious and terrible to look. But the wolves began to pursue those sheep until they reached a sea of water. That sea was divided, and the water stood on this side and on that before them, and their Lord led them and placed himself between them and the wolves. As the wolves did not yet see the sheep, they proceeded into the middle of that sea, and the wolves followed the sheep into that sea. When they saw the lord of the sheep, they turned to flee before his face, but that sea gathered itself together, and became as it had been created, and the water swelled and rose until it covered the wolves. I watched until all the wolves who pursued those sheep perished and were drowned."

"The sheep escaped from that water and went out into a wilderness, where there was no water and no grass, and they began to open their eyes and to see, and I saw the Lord of the sheep feeding them and giving them water and grass, and that sheep leading them. That sheep ascended to the summit of that lofty rock, and the Lord of the sheep went to them. Then I saw the Lord of the sheep stood before them, and his appearance was great and terrible and majestic, and all those sheep saw him and were afraid before him. They were all afraid and trembled because of him, and they cried to that sheep with them, 'We are not able to stand before our Lord or at look him.'"

"That sheep who led them, again ascended to the summit of that rock, but the sheep became blind and wandered from the way which he had shown them, but that sheep did not know it. The Lord of the sheep was irate, and that sheep found out and went down from the summit of the rock, and returned to the sheep, and found the majority of them blinded and wandering away. When they saw it, they were afraid and trembled at its presence, and desired to return to their folds. That sheep took other sheep with it, and came to those sheep which had wandered away, and began to murder them, and the sheep were terrified in its presence, and so that sheep brought back those sheep that had wandered away and they returned to their folds."

"I watched this dream until that sheep became a man and built a house for the Lord of the sheep, and placed all the sheep in that house. I watched until this sheep which had met that sheep which led them fell asleep, and I saw until all the great sheep perished and little ones arose in their place, and they came to a pasture, and approached a stream of water. Then that sheep, their leader which had become a man, withdrew from them and fell asleep, and all the sheep searched for it and mourned greatly because of it."

"I watched until they stopped crying for that sheep and crossed that stream of water, and there rose the two sheep as leaders in the place of those which had led them and fallen asleep. I watched until the sheep came to a good place, and a pleasant and glorious land, and I watched until those sheep were satisfied, and that house stood among them in the pleasant land."

"Sometimes their eyes were opened, and sometimes blinded, until another sheep arose and led them and brought them all back, and their eyes were opened. The dog and the foxes and the wild boars began to devour those sheep until the Lord of the sheep raised up another sheep as ram among them, who led them. That ram began to butt on either side those dog, foxes, and wild boars until he had destroyed them all. That sheep whose eyes were opened saw that ram, who was among the sheep, until it forgot its glory and began to butt those sheep, and trampled on them, and behaved unseemly. The Lord of the sheep sent to the lamb another lamb and raised it to being a ram and leader of the sheep instead of that ram which had forgotten its glory. It went to it and spoke to it alone, and raised it to being a ram, and made it the prince and leader of the sheep, but during all these things those dog oppressed the sheep. The first ram chased that second ram, and that second ram arose and fled before it, and I watched those dog pulled down the first ram. That second ram arose and led the little sheep. Those sheep grew and multiplied, but all the dogs, and foxes, and wild boars were afraid and fled before it, and that ram butted and killed the wild beasts, and those wild beasts no longer had any power among the sheep and did not rob them again. That ram fathered many sheep and fell asleep, and a little sheep became ram in its place, and became prince and leader of those sheep."

"That house became great and broad, and it was built for those sheep, and a tower lofty and great was built on the house for the Lord of the sheep, and that house was low. The tower was elevated and lofty, and the Lord of the sheep stood on that tower and they offered a full table before him."

"Again I saw those sheep that they again erred and went many ways, and forgot that their houses, and the Lord of the sheep called some from among the sheep and sent them to the sheep, but the sheep began to murder them. One of them was saved and was not killed, and it ran away and cried loudly over the sheep, and they wanted to kill it, but the Lord of the sheep saved it from the sheep, and brought it up to me, and caused it to live here."

"He sent many other sheep to those sheep to testify to them and lament over them. After that I saw that when they forgot the house of the Lord and his tower, they were lost entirely, and their eyes were blinded, and I saw the Lord of the sheep, how he caused a great deal of slaughter among them in their herds until those sheep that invited that slaughter, betrayed his place. He gave them over into the hands of the lions and tigers, and wolves and hyenas, and into the hand of the foxes, and to all the wild beasts, and those wild beasts began to tear into pieces those sheep. I saw that he forgot their house and their tower and gave them all into the hand of the lions, to tear and devour them, into the hand of all the wild beasts. I began to cry aloud with all my power, and to appeal to the Lord of the sheep, and to represent to him in regard to the sheep that they were devoured by all the wild beasts. But he remained unmoved, and he watched it and celebrated that they were devoured and swallowed and robbed, and left them to be devoured in the hand of all the beasts."

"He called seventy shepherds, and sent those sheep to them that they might pasture them, and he spoke to the shepherds and their companions, 'Let each of you pasture the sheep from now on, and everything I command you, you will do. I will give them to you already counted, and tell you which of them are to be destroyed, and you will destroy them.'"

"He gave over those sheep to them. He called another and said him, 'Observe and record everything that the shepherds will do to those sheep, in case they kill more of them than I have commanded them. Every excess and destruction which will be worked through the shepherds, record how many they destroy according to my command, and how many according to their own desire. Record every individual shepherd, all the slaughter he does. Read out before me by number how many they slaughter, and how many they deliver over for destruction, that I may have this as a testimony against them, and know every deed of the shepherds, that I may comprehend and see what they do, whether or not they stay by my command which I have commanded them. But they will not know it, and you will not tell it to them, or admonish them, but only record regarding each individual all the slaughter which the shepherds effect each in his time and lays it all before me.'"

"I watched until those shepherds pastured in their season, and they began to slay and to destroy more than they were commanded, and they delivered those sheep into the hand of the lions. The lions and tigers eat and devoured the greater part of those sheep, and the wild boars eat along with them, and they burnt that tower and demolished that house. I became exceedingly sorrowful over that tower because that house of the sheep was demolished, and afterward I was unable to see those sheep entered that house."

"The shepherds and their associates gave over those sheep to all the wild beasts, to devour them, and each one of them received in his time a definite number. It was written by the other in a book how many each one of them slaughtered. Each one killed and destroyed many more than was commanded, and I began to cry and lament on account of those sheep. So in the vision I saw that one who wrote, how he wrote down everyone that was destroyed by those shepherds, day by day, and carried up and laid down and showed actually the whole book to the Lord of the sheep, everything that they had done, and all that each one of them had made away with, and all that they had given over to destruction. The book was read before the Lord of the sheep, and he took the book from his hand and read it and sealed it and laid it down."

"Immediately I saw how the shepherds pastured for twelve hours, and saw three of those sheep turned back and came and entered and began to build up all that had fallen down of that house, but the wild boars tried to delay them, yet were unable. They again began to build like before, and they built up that tower, and it was named the high tower, and they began again to place a table before the tower, but all the bread on it was polluted and impure. In regards to all this, the eyes of those sheep were blinded so that they didn't see, and their shepherds also. They delivered large numbers of them to their shepherds for slaughter, and they trampled the sheep with their feet and devoured them. The Lord of the sheep remained unmoved until all the sheep were dispersed over the field and mingled with them, and they did not save them out of the hand of the beasts."

"The one who wrote the book carried it up, and showed it and read it before the Lord of the sheep, and begged him on their account as he showed him all the doings of the shepherds, and gave witness against all the shepherds before him. He took the actual book and laid it down beside him and departed."

Dream Visions - Chapter 7 Interpreted

"ONE OF THOSE FOUR WENT to that white bull and instructed him in a secret, without his being terrified. Even though he was born a bull, he became a man, [Noah] and built for himself a great vessel and lived in it, and three bulls lived with him in that vessel, and they were covered within it. I raised my eyes towards the sky again and saw a high ceiling, with seven water torrents in it, and those torrents flowed great floods into a reservoir."

"I looked again and saw fountains opened on the surface of that great reservoir, and the water began to full up and rise to the surface, and I watched that reservoir until all its surface was covered with water. The water, the darkness, and mist increased on it, and as I observed the height of that water, that water rose above the height of the reservoir, and was streaming over the edge of the reservoir, and it fell on the Earth. All the livestock crowded together until I saw how they sank and were swallowed up and drowned in that water. But that vessel floated on the water, while all the oxen and elephants and camels and donkeys sank to the bottom with all the animals, so that I could no longer see them, and they were not able to escape but drowned and sank into the depths."

"I continued to dream until those water torrents were removed from that high ceiling, and the chasms of the Earth were filled in and other abysses were opened. Then the water began to run down into these, until the Earth became visible, and that vessel settled on the Earth, and the darkness left and light appeared. Noah [That white bull which had become a man] came out of that vessel, and the three bulls with him, and one of those three was Japheth [white like that bull], and one of them was Shem [red as blood], and one Ham [black], and Noah [that white bull] departed from them."

"They began to bring out the domesticated animals and birds, so that there arose different kinds: lions, tigers, wolves, dogs, hyenas, wild boars, foxes, squirrels, hogs, falcons, vultures, kites, eagles, and ravens, and among them was born a white bull. They began to bite one another, but Japheth [that white bull which was born among them] fathered a wild donkey and Abraham [a white bull] along with them. The wild donkeys multiplied, but Abraham [that bull] which was born from him fathered Esau [a black wild boar] and Isaac [a white sheep], and the former fathered many boars, but that sheep fathered twelve patriarchs [sheep]. When those twelve patriarchs [sheep] had grown, they gave up Joseph [one of them] to the Midianites [donkeys], and those Midianites [donkeys] again gave up Joseph [that sheep] to the Egyptians [wolves], and Joseph [that sheep] grew up among the Egyptians [wolves]."

"The Lord brought the eleven patriarchs [sheep] to live with Joseph [it] and to pasture with Joseph [it] among the Egyptians [wolves], and they multiplied and became Israel [many flocks of sheep.] The Egyptians [wolves] began to fear them, and they oppressed them until they destroyed their little ones, and they threw their young into the Nile [a river of great water], but those sheep began to cry out loud on account of their little ones, and to complain to their Lord. Moses [A sheep] which had been saved from the Egyptians [wolves] fled and escaped to the Midianites [wild donkeys], and I saw Israel [the sheep] and how they lamented and cried, and begged their Lord with all their might, until that Lord of Israel [the sheep] descended to the voices of Israel [the sheep] from a lofty home, and came to them and fed them."

"He called Moses [that sheep] who [which] had escaped the Egyptians [wolves], and spoke with it concerning the Egyptians [wolves] that it should admonish them not to touch Israel [the sheep]. Moses [The sheep] went to the Egyptians [wolves] obeying to the commands of the Lord, and Aaron [another sheep] met him [it] and went with him [it], and the two went and entered together into the assembly of those Egyptians [wolves], and spoke with them and admonished them to not touch Israel [the sheep] from from then on. On hearing it, I saw the Egyptians [wolves] and how they oppressed Israel [the sheep] greatly with all their power, and Israel [the sheep] cried aloud."

"The Lord came to Israel [the sheep] and they began to kill the Egyptians [wolves], and the Egyptians [wolves] began to cry but Israel [the sheep] became quiet and immediately stopped crying out. I watched Israel [the sheep] until they departed from among the Egyptians [wolves], but the eyes of the Egyptians [wolves] were blinded, and those Egyptians [wolves] departed in pursuit of Israel [the sheep] with all their power. The Lord of Israel [the sheep] went with them as their leader, and all his sheep followed him, and his face was dazzling and glorious and terrible to look. But the Egyptians [wolves] began to pursue those sheep until they reached the Red Sea [a sea of water]. That sea was divided, and the water stood on this side and on that before them, and their Lord led them and placed himself between them and the Egyptians [wolves]. As the Egyptians [wolves] did not yet see Israel [the sheep], they proceeded into the middle of that sea, and the Egyptians [wolves] followed Israel [the sheep] into that sea. When they saw the lord of Israel [the sheep], they turned to flee before his face, but that sea gathered itself together, and became as it had been created, and the water swelled and rose until it covered the Egyptians [wolves]. I watched until all the Egyptians [wolves] who pursued those sheep perished and were drowned."

"Israel [the sheep] escaped from that water and went out into a wilderness, where there was no water and no grass, and they began to open their eyes and to see, and I saw the Lord of Israel [the sheep] feeding them and giving them water and grass, and Moses [that sheep] leading them. Moses [That sheep] ascended to the summit of Mount Sinai or Horeb [that lofty rock], and the Lord of Israel [the sheep] went to them. Then I saw the Lord of Israel [the sheep] stood before them, and his appearance was great and terrible and majestic, and all the Israelite [those sheep] saw him and were afraid before him. They were all afraid and trembled because of him, and they cried to Moses [that sheep] with them, 'We are not able to stand before our Lord or at look him.'"

"Moses [That sheep] who led them, again ascended to the summit Mount Sinai or Horeb [of that rock], but Israel [the sheep] became blind and wandered from the way which he had shown them, but Moses [that sheep] did not know it. The Lord of Israel [the sheep] was irate, and Moses [that sheep] found out and went down from Mount Sinai or Horeb [the summit of the rock], and returned to Israel [the sheep], and found the majority of them blinded and wandering away. When they saw Moses [it], they were afraid and trembled at Moses' [its] presence, and desired to return to their folds. Moses [That sheep] took other Israelites [sheep] with him [it], and came to those Israelites [sheep] who [which] had wandered away, and began to murder them, and Israel [the sheep] were terrified in Moses' [its] presence, and so Moses [that sheep] brought back those Israelites [sheep] that had wandered away and they returned to their folds."

"I watched this dream until Moses [that sheep] became a man and built a tabernacle [house] for the Lord of Israel [the sheep], and placed all Israel [the sheep] in that house. I watched until Aaron [this sheep which had met that sheep which led them] died [fell asleep], and I saw until all the older Israelites [great sheep] perished and little ones arose in their place, and they came to a pasture, and approached the Jordan River [a stream of water]. Then Moses [that sheep], their leader who [which] had become a man, withdrew from them and died [fell asleep], and all Israel [the sheep] searched for him [it] and mourned greatly because of him [it]."

"I watched until they stopped crying for Moses [that sheep] and crossed the Jordan River [that stream of water], and there rose Joshua and Eleazar [the two sheep as leaders] in the place of those who [which] had led them and died [fallen asleep]. I watched until Israel [the sheep] came to a good place, and a pleasant and glorious land, and I watched until the Israelite [those sheep] were satisfied, and the tabernacle [that house] stood among them in the pleasant land."

"Sometimes their eyes were opened, and sometimes blinded, until another prophet [sheep] arose and led them and brought them all back, and their eyes were opened. The Philistines [dogs[D6]] and the foxes and the wild boars began to devour the Israelites [those sheep] until the Lord of Israel [the sheep] raised up another prophet [sheep] as king [ram] from among them, who led them. Saul [That ram] began to butt on either side those Philistines [dogs], foxes, and wild boars until he had destroyed them all. Samuel [That sheep whose eyes were opened] saw Saul [that ram], who was among Israel [the sheep], until he [it] forgot his [its] glory and began to butt the Israelites [those sheep], and trampled on them, and behaved unseemly. The Lord of Israel [the sheep] sent to Samuel [the lamb] David [another lamb] and raised him [it] to being a king [ram] and leader of Israel [the sheep] instead of Saul [that ram] who [which] had forgotten his [its] glory. Samuel [It] went to David [it] and spoke to it alone, and raised David [it] to being a king [ram], and made David [it] the prince and leader of Israel [the sheep], but during all these things those Philistines [dogs] oppressed Israel [the sheep]. Saul [The first ram] chased David [that second ram], and David [that second ram] arose and fled before it, and I watched those Philistines [dogs] pulled down Saul [the first ram]. David [That second ram] arose and led the Israelites [little sheep]. Israel [Those sheep] grew and multiplied, but all the Philistines [dogs], and foxes, and wild boars were afraid and fled before Israel [it], and David [that ram] butted and killed the wild beasts, and those wild beasts no longer had any power among Israel [the sheep] and did not rob them again. David [That ram] fathered many sheep and died [fell asleep], and Solomon [a little sheep] became king [ram] in his [its] place, and became prince and leader of Israel [those sheep]."

"That temple [house] became great and broad, and it was built for those sheep, and a tower lofty and great was built on the temple [house] for the Lord of Israel [the sheep], and that house was low. The tower was elevated and lofty, and the Lord of Israel [the sheep] stood on that tower and they offered a full table before him."

"Again I saw those sheep that they again erred and went many ways, and forgot that their houses, and the Lord of Israel [the sheep] called some from among Israel [the sheep] and sent them to Israel [the sheep], but Israel [the sheep] began to murder them. Elijah [One of them] was saved and was not killed, and he [it] ran away and cried loudly over Israel [the sheep], and they wanted to kill him [it], but the Lord of Israel [the sheep] saved Elijah [it] from Israel [the sheep], and brought him [it] up to me, and caused him [it] to live here."

"He sent many other prophets [sheep] to Israeli [those sheep] to testify to them and lament over them. After that I saw that when they forgot the temple [house] of the Lord and his tower, they were lost entirely, and their eyes were blinded, and I saw the Lord of Israel [the sheep], how he caused a great deal of slaughter among them in their herds until those sheep that invited that slaughter, betrayed his place. He gave them over into the hands of the Babylonians [lions[D7]] and tigers, and Egyptians [wolves] and hyenas, and into the hand of the foxes, and to all the wild beasts, and those wild beasts began to tear into pieces those sheep. I saw that he forgot their temple [house] and their tower and gave them all into the hand of the Babylonians [lions], to tear and devour them, into the hand of all the wild beasts. I began to cry aloud with all my power, and to appeal to the Lord of Israel [the sheep], and to represent to him in regard to Israel [the sheep] that they were devoured by all the wild beasts. But he remained unmoved, and he watched it and celebrated that they were devoured and swallowed and robbed, and left them to be devoured in the hand of all the beasts."

"He called seventy priests [shepherds], and sent those prophets [sheep] to them that they might lead [pasture] them, and he spoke to the priests [shepherds] and their companions, 'Let each of you pasture Israel [the sheep] from now on, and everything I command you, you will do. I will give them to you already counted, and tell you which of them are to be destroyed, and you will destroy them.'"

"He gave over Israel [those sheep] to them. He called another and said him, 'Observe and record everything that the priests [shepherds] will do to Israel [those sheep], in case they kill more of them than I have commanded them. Every excess and destruction which will be worked through the priests [shepherds], record how many they destroy according to my command, and how many according to their own desire. Record every individual priest [shepherd], all the slaughter he does. Read out before me by number how many they slaughter, and how many they deliver over for destruction, that I may have this as a testimony against them, and know every deed of the priests [shepherds], that I may comprehend and see what they do, whether or not they stay by my command which I have commanded them. But they will not know it, and you will not tell it to them, or admonish them, but only record regarding each individual all the slaughter which the priests [shepherds] effect each in his time and lays it all before me.'"

"I watched until those priests [shepherds] pastured in their season, and they began to slay and to destroy more than they were commanded, and they delivered those sheep into the hand of the Babylonians [lions]. The Babylonians [lions] and tigers eat and devoured the greater part of those sheep, and the wild boars eat along with them, and they burnt that tower and demolished that house. I became exceedingly sorrowful over that tower because that house of Israel [the sheep] was demolished, and afterward I was unable to see Israel [those sheep] entered that house."

"The priests [shepherds] and their associates gave over Israel [those sheep] to all the wild beasts, to devour them, and each one of them received in his time a definite number. It was written by the other in a book how many each one of them slaughtered. Each one killed and destroyed many more than was commanded, and I began to cry and lament on account of those sheep. So in the vision I saw that one who wrote, how he wrote down everyone that was destroyed by those priests [shepherds], day by day, and carried up and laid down and showed actually the whole book to the Lord of Israel [the sheep], everything that they had done, and all that each one of them had made away with, and all that they had given over to destruction. The book was read before the Lord of Israel [the sheep], and he took the book from his hand and read it and sealed it and laid it down."

"Immediately I saw how the priests [shepherds] pastured for twelve hours, and saw three of Israel [those sheep] turned back and came and entered and began to build up all that had fallen down of that house, but the wild boars tried to delay them, yet were unable. They again began to build like before, and they built up that tower, and it was named the high tower, and they began again to place a table before the tower, but all the bread on it was polluted and impure. In regards to all this, the eyes of Israel [those sheep] were blinded so that they didn't see, and their priests [shepherds] also. They delivered large numbers of them to their priests [shepherds] for slaughter, and they trampled Israel [the sheep] with their feet and devoured them. The Lord of Israel [the sheep] remained unmoved until all Israel [the sheep] were dispersed over the field and mingled with them, and they did not save them out of the hand of the beasts."

"The one who wrote the book carried it up, and showed it and read it before the Lord of Israel [the sheep], and begged him on their account as he showed him all the doings of the priests [shepherds], and gave witness against all the priests [shepherds] before him. He took the actual book and laid it down beside him and departed."

Dream Visions - Chapter 8

———

"I WATCHED UNTIL THIRTY-five shepherds went out to pasture, and they ended their times as severally as the first, and others took them to pasture for some time, each shepherd in his own time."

"Then I saw in my dream all the birds of the sky coming, the eagles, the vultures, the kites, and the ravens. The eagles led all the birds, and they began to devour those sheep, and to pick out their eyes and to devour their flesh. The sheep cried out because their flesh was being devoured by the birds, and I watched and lamented in my sleep for that shepherd who pastured the sheep. I watched those sheep being devoured by the dogs and eagles and kites, and they left no flesh, skin, or sinew remaining on them until only their bones stood there, and their bones too fell to the Earth and the sheep became few."

"I saw that twenty-three had gone out to pasture and completed in their several periods fifty-eight years. Then I saw that lambs were born to those white sheep, and they began to open their eyes and to see, and to cry to the sheep. Yes, they cried to them, but they did not listen to what they said to them, but were completely deaf, and their eyes were completely blind. I saw in the dream how the ravens flew on those lambs and took those lambs, and dashed the sheep into pieces and eat them. I saw horns grew on those lambs, and the ravens knocked down their horns."

"I saw a great horn grew on one of those sheep, and their eyes were opened. It looked at them and their eyes opened, and it cried to the sheep, and the rams saw it and all ran to it. Nevertheless, all this those eagles and vultures and ravens and kites still kept tearing the sheep and swooping down on them and devouring them, yet the sheep remained silent, but the rams lamented and cried out. Those ravens fought and battled with it and wanted to tear down its horn, but they had no power over it."

"I saw the shepherds and eagles and those vultures and kites came, and they cried to the ravens that they should break the horn of that ram, and they battled and fought with it, and it battled with them and cried that its help might come. All the eagles and vultures and ravens and kites were gathered together, and there came with them all the sheep of the field, yes, they all came together, and helped each other to break that horn of the ram."

"I saw a great sword was given to the sheep, and the sheep proceeded against all the beasts of the field to slay them, and all the beasts and the birds of the sky fled before their face. I saw till that man, who wrote down the names of the shepherds and carried up into the presence of the Lord of the sheep came and helped and showed it everything. He had come down for the help of that ram. I saw that man, who wrote the book according to the command of the Lord opened that book concerning the destruction which those twelve last shepherds had worked, and showed that they had slaughtered much more than their predecessors, before the Lord of the sheep."

"I saw the Lord of the sheep came to them in anger, and all who saw him fled, and they all fell into his shadow from before his face."

"I saw the Lord of the sheep came to them and took in his hand the staff of anger, and hit the Earth, and the Earth was smashed apart, and all the beasts and all the birds of the sky fell from among those sheep, and were swallowed up in the Earth and it covered them."

"I saw a throne was erected in the pleasant land, and the Lord of the sheep sat himself on it, and the other took the sealed books and opened those books before the Lord of the sheep. The Lord called those men the seven first white ones, and commanded that they should bring before him, beginning with the first star which led the way, all the stars whose genitals were like those of horses, and they brought them all before him. He said to that man who wrote before him, being one of those seven white ones, 'Bring those seventy shepherds to who I delivered the sheep, and who taking them on their own authority killed more than I commanded them.'"

"They were all bound, and I saw them stand before him. The judgment was decided first over the stars, and they were judged and found guilty, and went to the place of condemnation, and they were cast into an abyss full of fire and flame, and pillars of fire. Those seventy shepherds were judged and found guilty, and they were thrown into that fiery abyss. I saw at that time how a similar abyss was opened in the Earth, full of fire, and they brought those blind sheep, and they were all judged and found guilty and thrown into this fiery abyss, and they burned, now this abyss was to the right of that house. I saw those sheep burning and their bones burning. I stood up to watch as they packed up that old house, and carried off all the pillars, and all the beams. The ornaments of the house were packed up with it at the same time, and they carried it off and laid it in a place in the south of the land."

"I saw the Lord of the sheep brought a new house greater and loftier than the first, and set it up in the place of the first which had been packed up. All its pillars were new, and its ornaments were new and larger than those of the first, the old one which he had taken away, and all the sheep were within it."

"I saw all the sheep which had been left, and all the beasts on the Earth, and all the birds of the sky, falling down and doing homage to those sheep and making petitions and obeying them in everything. Then, those three who were clothed in white and had seized me by my hand and had taken me up previously, along with the hand of that ram also grabbing hold of me, took me up and set me down among those sheep before the judgment took place. Those sheep were all white, and their wool was abundant and clean. All that had been destroyed and dispersed, and all the beasts of the field, and all the birds of the sky, assembled in that house, and the Lord of the sheep rejoiced with great celebration because they were all good and had returned to his house."

"I saw them lay down that sword that had been given to the sheep, and they brought it back into the house, and it was sealed before the presence of the Lord, and all the sheep were invited into that house, but it could not hold them. All their eyes were opened, and they saw well, and there was not one among them that did not see."

"I saw that that house was large and broad and very full."

"I saw that a white bull was born, with large horns and all the beasts of the field and all the birds of the air were afraid him and made petition to him all the time. I saw all their generations were transformed, and they all became white bulls, and the first among them became a lamb, and that lamb became a great animal and had great black horns on its head, and the Lord of the sheep rejoiced over it and over all the oxen."

I awoke and remembered everything. This is the dream I saw while I slept, and I awoke and blessed the Lord of righteousness and gave him glory. Then I wept with a great weeping and my tears did not stop until I could no longer endure it. My tears flowed because of what I had seen, for everything will happen and be fulfilled, and all the deeds of men in their order were showed to me. In that night, I remembered the first dream, and because of it I wept and was troubled, because I had seen that dream."

Dream Visions - Chapter 8 Interpreted

"I WATCHED UNTIL THIRTY-five priests [shepherds] went out to lead [pasture], and they ended their times as terribly as the first, and others took them to pasture for some time, each priest [shepherd] in his own time."

"Then I saw in my dream all the birds of the sky coming, the Persians [eagles[D8]], the vultures, the kites, and the ravens. The Persians [eagles] led all the birds, and they began to devour Israel [those sheep], and to pick out their eyes and to devour their flesh. Israel [the sheep] cried out because their flesh was being devoured by the birds, and I watched and lamented in my sleep for that priest [shepherd] who pastured Israel [the sheep]. I watched those sheep being devoured by the Philistines [dogs] and Persians [eagles] and kites, and they left no flesh, skin, or sinew remaining on them until only their bones stood there, and their bones too fell to the Earth and Israel [the sheep] became few."

"I saw that twenty-three had gone out to pasture and completed in their several periods fifty-eight years. Then I saw that lambs were born to those white sheep, and they began to open their eyes and to see, and to cry to Israel [the sheep]. Yes, they cried to them, but they did not listen to what they said to them, but were completely deaf, and their eyes were completely blind. I saw in the dream how the ravens flew on those lambs and took those lambs, and dashed Israel [the sheep] into pieces and eat them. I saw horns grew on those lambs, and the ravens knocked down their horns."

"I saw a great horn grew on one of those sheep, and their eyes were opened. It looked at them and their eyes opened, and it cried to Israel [the sheep], and the kings [rams] saw it and all ran to it. Nevertheless, all this those Persians [eagles] and vultures and ravens and kites still kept tearing Israel [the sheep] and swooping down on them and devouring them, yet Israel [the sheep] remained silent, but the kings [rams] lamented and cried out. Those ravens fought and battled with it and wanted to tear down its horn, but they had no power over it."

"I saw the priests [shepherds] and Persians [eagles] and those vultures and kites came, and they cried to the ravens that they should break the horn of that king [ram], and they battled and fought with it, and it battled with them and cried that its help might come. All the Persians [eagles] and vultures and ravens and kites were gathered together, and there came with them all Israel [the sheep] of the field, yes, they all came together, and helped each other to break that horn of the king [ram]."

"I saw a great sword was given to Israel [the sheep], and Israel [the sheep] proceeded against all the beasts of the field to slay them, and all the beasts and the birds of the sky fled before their face. I saw till that man, who wrote down the names of the priests [shepherds] and carried up into the presence of the Lord of Israel [the sheep] came and helped and showed it everything. He had come down for the help of that king [ram]. I saw that man, who wrote the book according to the command of the Lord opened that book concerning the destruction which those twelve last priests [shepherds] had worked, and showed that they had slaughtered much more than their predecessors, before the Lord of Israel [the sheep]."

"I saw the Lord of Israel [the sheep] came to them in anger, and all who saw him fled, and they all fell into his shadow from before his face."

"I saw the Lord of Israel [the sheep] came to them and took in his hand the staff of anger, and hit the Earth, and the Earth was smashed apart, and all the beasts and all the birds of the sky fell from among those sheep, and were swallowed up in the Earth and it covered them."

"I saw a throne was erected in the pleasant land, and the Lord of Israel [the sheep] sat himself on it, and the other took the sealed books and opened those books before the Lord of Israel [the sheep]. The Lord called those men the seven first white ones, and commanded that they should bring before him, beginning with the first star which led the way, all the stars whose genitals were like those of horses, and they brought them all before him. He said to that man who wrote before him, being one of those seven white ones, 'Bring those seventy priests [shepherds] to who I delivered Israel [the sheep], and who taking them on their own authority killed more than I commanded them.'"

"They were all bound, and I saw them stand before him. The judgment was decided first over the stars, and they were judged and found guilty, and went to the place of condemnation, and they were cast into an abyss full of fire and flame, and pillars of fire. Those seventy priests [shepherds] were judged and found guilty, and they were thrown into that fiery abyss. I saw at that time how a similar abyss was opened in the Earth, full of fire, and they brought those blind sheep, and they were all judged and found guilty and thrown into this fiery abyss, and they burned, now this abyss was to the right of that house. I saw those sheep burning and their bones burning. I stood up to watch as they packed up that old house, and carried off all the pillars, and all the beams. The ornaments of the house were packed up with it at the same time, and they carried it off and laid it in a place in the south of the land."

"I saw the Lord of Israel [the sheep] brought a new house greater and loftier than the first, and set it up in the place of the first which had been packed up. All its pillars were new, and its ornaments were new and larger than those of the first, the old one which he had taken away, and all Israel [the sheep] were within it."

"I saw all Israel [the sheep] which had been left, and all the beasts on the Earth, and all the birds of the sky, falling down and doing homage to those sheep and making petitions and obeying them in everything. Then, those three who were clothed in white and had seized me by my hand and had taken me up previously, along with the hand of that king [ram] also grabbing hold of me, took me up and set me down among those sheep before the judgment took place. Those sheep were all white, and their wool was abundant and clean. All that had been destroyed and dispersed, and all the beasts of the field, and all the birds of the sky, assembled in that house, and the Lord of Israel [the sheep] rejoiced with great celebration because they were all good and had returned to his house."

"I saw them lay down that sword that had been given to Israel [the sheep], and they brought it back into the house, and it was sealed before the presence of the Lord, and all Israel [the sheep] were invited into that house, but it could not hold them. All their eyes were opened, and they saw well, and there was not one among them that did not see."

"I saw that that house was large and broad and very full."

"I saw that a white bull was born, with large horns and all the beasts of the field and all the birds of the air were afraid him and made petition to him all the time. I saw all their generations were transformed, and they all became white bulls, and the first among them became a lamb, and that lamb became a great animal and had great black horns on its head, and the Lord of Israel [the sheep] rejoiced over it and over all the oxen."

I awoke and remembered everything. This is the dream I saw while I slept, and I awoke and blessed the Lord of righteousness and gave him glory. Then I wept with a great weeping and my tears did not stop until I could no longer endure it. My tears flowed because of what I had seen, for everything will happen and be fulfilled, and all the deeds of men in their order were showed to me. In that night, I remembered the first dream, and because of it I wept and was troubled, because I had seen that dream."

Letter of Enoch - Chapter 1

———

[ENOCH SAID,] "NOW, my son Methuselah, call your brothers to me all and gather all the sons of your mother. The Word[L1] calls me, and the spirit is poured out on me, so I may show you everything that will befall you forever."

Methuselah left and called all his brothers to him and assembled his relatives.

He spoke to all the children of righteousness[L2] and said, "Hear, sons of Enoch, all the words of your father, and listen to the voice of my mouth. I exhort you and say to you, beloved, 'Love uprightness and follow closely. Don't draw near to uprightness with a duplicitous heart, and don't associate with those with a duplicitous heart, but continue in righteousness, my sons. It will guide you along good paths, and righteousness will be your companion. I know that violence will increase on the Earth, and a great punishment be executed on the Earth, and all unrighteousness will come to an end. It will be cut off from its roots, and its whole structure will be destroyed."

"Unrighteousness will return to the Earth, and all the unrighteousness deeds, violence, and transgression will double. When sin, unrighteousness, blasphemy, and violence of all kinds increases, and apostasy, transgression, and uncleanness increases, a great punishment will come from the sky on all these, and the Holy Lord[L3] will come out in anger to execute judgment and punishment on Earth. In those days, violence will be cut off from its roots, and the roots of unrighteousness and deceit will be destroyed from under the sky. All the idols of the heathens will be abandoned, and the temples burned with fire. They will remove them from the whole Earth, and they will be thrown into the judgment fire, and will be permanently destroyed in an angry and terrible judgment."

"The righteous will rise from their sleep, and Wisdom[L4] will rise and be given to them. Then the roots of unrighteousness will be cut off, and the sinners will be destroyed by the sword [... missing text ...] will be cut off from the blasphemers in every place, and those who plan violence and those who commit blasphemy will be killed by the sword."

"Then there will be another week, the eighth week,[L5] one of righteousness, when a sword will be given to the righteous so judgment may be executed on the oppressors, and sinners will be delivered into the hands of the righteous. In the end, the righteousness will acquire houses, and a house will be built for the great King of Glory[L6] forever, and all mankind will follow the upright path."

"After that, in the ninth week,[L7] the righteous judgment will be revealed to the whole world, and all the works of the godless will vanish from all the Earth, and the world will be marked down for destruction."

"After this, in the tenth week on the seventh day,[L8] there will come the great final judgment, in which he will execute vengeance among the watchers. The first the sky will leave and pass away, and a new the sky will appear, and all the powers of the skies will give seven times brighter.[9] After that, there will be many weeks without number forever, and all will be in goodness and righteousness, and sin will no longer exist forever. I tell you my sons and will show you the paths of righteousness and the paths of violence. Yes, I will tell you them again, so you will know what will happen. Now, listen to me, my sons, and follow in the paths of righteousness, and don't follow to the paths of violence. For all who walk in the paths of unrighteousness will die forever."

Letter of Enoch - Chapter 2

THE BOOK WRITTEN BY Enoch, Enoch wrote this complete book of wisdom, praised by all men and a judge of all the Earth for all my children who will live on the Earth. For the future generations who will observe uprightness and peace.

Don't let your spirit be troubled because of the account of the times. The Holy Great One has planed days for all things. The righteous one will rise from sleep, will rise and walk in the paths of righteousness, and all his path and conversation will be in eternal goodness and grace. He will be gracious to the righteous and give him eternal uprightness, and he will give him power so that he will be endowed with goodness and righteousness. He will walk in eternal light.

Sin will die in darkness forever, and will no more be seen from that day forever.

Letter of Enoch - Chapter 3

AFTER THAT, ENOCH BOTH gave the books and began to read from the books.

Enoch said, "I will speak of the children of righteousness, and the chosen of the world, and the plant of uprightness. I, Enoch, say to you my sons, according to what I saw in my the heavenly vision, and which I have been told through by the holy watchers, and have learned from the heavenly tablets."

Enoch read from the books, "I was born the seventh[L9] in the first week,[L10] when judgment and righteousness still endured. After me, great wickedness and deceit will rise in the second week."[L11]

"In it there will be the first end, and in it a man will be saved.[L12] After it has ended unrighteousness will grow up, and a law will be made for the sinners. After that, at the end of the third week[L13] a man will be chosen as the seed of righteous judgment, and his posterity will become the seed of righteousness forever."

"After that in the fourth week, at its close, visions of the holy and righteous will be seen, and a law for all generations and an enclosure will be made for them."[L14]

"After that in the fifth week, at its close, the house of glory and dominion will be built forever."[L15]

"After that in the sixth week all who live in it will be blinded, and the hearts of all of them will godlessly forsake wisdom. In it, a man will ascend. At its close, the house of dominion will be burnt with fire, and the whole race of the chosen root will be dispersed."[L16]

"After that, in the seventh week, an apostate generation will rise, and many will be its deeds, and all its deeds will be apostate."[L17]

"At its close will be selected the chosen righteous of the eternal seed of righteousness, to receive seven times instruction concerning all his creation."

"For who is there of all the children of men that can hear the voice of the holy one without being troubled? Who can think his thoughts? Who is there that can see all the works of the sky? How should there be one who could see the sky, and who is there that could understand the things of the sky and see a mind or a spirit and could describe it, or ascend and see all their ends and be like them or do like them? Who is there of all men that could know what is the width and the length of the Earth? Who has been shown the measure of all of them? Is there anyone who could discern the length of the sky and how high it is, and what it is built on, or how many stars there are, and where all the luminaries rest?"

Letter of Enoch - Chapter 4

[ENOCH CONTINUED,] "I tell you, my sons, love righteousness and follow it, as the paths of righteousness are worthy of following, but the paths of unrighteousness will suddenly be destroyed and vanish. To certain men of a generation, the paths of violence and death will be revealed, and they will hold themselves far from them, and will not follow them. I speak to you, the righteous. Don't follow the paths of wickedness, or in the paths of death, and don't draw near to them in case you are destroyed. Choose righteousness and the life of the chosen, and follow in the paths of peace, and you will live and prosper."

"Keep my words in the thoughts of your hearts, and don't allow them to be removed from your hearts. I know that sinners will tempt men to treat Wisdom immorally, so no place may be found for her, and no manner of temptation may decrease."

"Woe to those who build unrighteousness and oppression and lay deceit as a foundation. For they will be suddenly overthrown, and they will have no peace."

"Woe to those who build their houses in sin, for from all their foundations will they be overthrown, and by the sword will they fall. Those who acquire gold and silver in judgment suddenly will die."

"Woe to you, you rich, for you have trusted in your riches, and from your riches will you leave, because you have not remembered the Highest in the days of your riches. You have committed blasphemy and unrighteousness, and have become ready for the day of slaughter, and the day of darkness and the day of the great judgment. Therefore I say to you, he who has created you will overthrow you, and for your fall there will be no compassion, and your creator will rejoice in your destruction."

"You righteous ones in those days will be a reproach to the sinners and the godless."

Letter of Enoch - Chapter 5

[ENOCH CONTINUED,] "IF only my eyes were a cloud of water! Then I might cry over you, and pour down my tears like a cloud of water. Then I might rest my troubled heart! Who has allowed you to practice reproaches and wickedness? Judgment will catch up to you, sinners! Don't be afraid of the sinners, you righteous. For again will the Lord will deliver them into your hands, that you may execute judgment on them according to your desires."

"Woe to you who curse in angry that which cannot be reversed. Healing will be far from you because of your sins. Woe to you who repay your neighbor with evil, for you will be repaid according to your works. Woe to you, lying witnesses, and to those who judge unjustly, for will you die suddenly. Woe to you, sinners, as you persecute the righteous. You will be delivered up and persecuted because of injustice, and it will weigh heavily on you."

Letter of Enoch - Chapter 6

[ENOCH CONTINUED,] "BE hopeful, you righteous, for suddenly the sinners will die before you, and you will rule over them according to your wishes. In the day of the tribulation of the sinners, your children will mount and rise as eagles, and higher than the vultures will be your nest, and you will ascend and enter the crevices of the Earth, and the clefts of the rock forever as coneys before the unrighteous, and the sirens[L18] will sigh because of you, and you will cry. So don't be afraid that you have suffered, as healing will be your reward. A bright light will enlighten you, and the voice of peace you will hear from the sky."

"Woe to you, you sinners, for your riches make you appear like the righteous, but your hearts convict you of being sinners, and this fact will be a testimony against you as a memorial of your evil deeds."

"Woe to you who eat the finest of the wheat, and drink wine in large bowls, and use your might to walk all over the poor. Woe to you who drink water from every fountain, because you will suddenly be consumed and wither away because you have forgotten the fountain of life. Woe to you who work unrighteousness and deceit and blasphemy. It will be recorded against you as evil. Woe to you, you mighty, who oppress the righteous. For the day of your destruction is coming. In those days, many good days will come to the righteous, in the day of your judgment."

Letter of Enoch - Chapter 7

[ENOCH CONTINUED,] "BELIEVE, you righteous, that the sinners will become a shame, and die in the day of unrighteousness."

"Know that the Highest will remember your destruction, and the watchers of the sky rejoice over your destruction. What will you do, you sinners, and where will you run on the day of judgment, when you hear the voice of the prayer of the righteous?"

"You will fare like those, against whom this letter will be a testimony. You have been companions of sinners. In those days the prayer of the righteous will reach the Lord, and for you, the days of your judgment will come. All the words of your unrighteousness will be read out before the Great Holy One, and your faces will be covered with shame, and he will reject every work which is grounded on unrighteousness."

"Woe to you sinners, who live on the sea or on the dry land, whose records are evil against you. Woe to you who acquire silver and gold in unrighteousness and say, 'We have become rich with riches and have possessions, and have acquired everything we have desired. Now let us do what we purposed. For we have gathered silver, and many are the shepherds in our houses. Our granaries are as full as with water.' Like water, your lies will flow away, for your riches will not remain but quickly leave you. You have acquired it all in unrighteousness, and you will be given over to a great curse."

Letter of Enoch - Chapter 8

[ENOCH CONTINUED,] "I swear to you, to both the wise and the fool, for you have diverse experiences on the Earth."

"You men will put on more adornments than a woman, brighter colored garments than a virgin, and in royalty and grandeur and power, and in silver, gold, purple[L19] in splendor. They will throw away food like water."

"They will be lacking in teachings and wisdom, and they will die with their possessions. With all their glory and their splendor, slaughtered in shame and great destitution, their spirits will be thrown into the furnace of fire. I have sworn to you, you sinners, as a mountain has not become a slave, and a hill does not become the handmaid of a woman, even so, sin has not been sent on the Earth, but man himself has created it, and they who commit it will fall under a great curse. Barrenness has not been given to the woman, but on account of the deeds of her own hands, she dies without children."

"I have sworn to you, you sinners, by the Holy Great One, that all your evil deeds are revealed in the skies, and that none of your deeds of oppression are covered and hidden. I have sworn to you, you sinners, by the Holy Great One, that all your evil deeds are revealed in the skies, and that none of your deeds of oppression are covered and hidden. From now on you know that all your oppression where you oppress is written down every day until the day of your judgment."

"Woe to you, you fools, for through your foolishness will you die. You transgress against the wise, and so good will not be your reward. Know you that you are prepared for the day of destruction. Do not hope to live, you sinners, but you will leave and die. You know no ransom, for you are prepared for the day of the great judgment, for the day of tribulation and a great shame for your spirits."

"Woe to you who are obstinate hearted, who work wickedness and eat blood. Where have you received good things to eat and to drink and to be filled? From all the good things which the Lord the Highest has placed in abundance on the Earth, therefore you will have no peace."

"Woe to you who love the deeds of unrighteousness, why do you hope for goodness only for yourselves? Know that you will be delivered into the hands of the righteous, and they will cut your necks and slay you and have no mercy on you."

"Woe to you who rejoice in the tribulation of the righteous, for no grave will be dug for you."

"Woe to you who dismiss the words of the righteous, for you have no hope of life."

"Woe to you who write down deceitful and godless words, for they write their lies so men may hear them and act godlessly towards their neighbor. Therefore they will have no peace but will die suddenly."

Letter of Enoch - Chapter 9

[ENOCH CONTINUED,] "WOE to you who work godlessness, and revel in lying and convincing them, 'You will die, and will not have a happy life.'"

"Woe to them who pervert the words of uprightness, and transgress the eternal law, and transform themselves into what they were not, into sinners. They will be trodden under foot on the Earth. Prepare in those days, you righteous, to raise your prayers like a memorial, and place them as a testimony before the watchers, that they may place the sin of the sinners as a memorial before the Highest. In those days the nations will be stirred up, and the families of the nations will rise on the day of destruction."

"In those days, the destitute will go out and carry off their children. They will abandon them, so that their children will die through them. They will abandon their sucklings babies, and not return to them, and have no pity on their beloved ones. Again, I swear to you, you sinners, that sin is prepared for a day of unceasing bloodshed. They who worship stones, and grave images of gold, silver, wood, stone, and clay, and those who worship impure spirits and demons, and all kinds of idols. They will get no kind of help or knowledge from them."

"They will become godless because of the foolishness of their hearts, and their eyes will be blinded through the fear of their hearts and through visions in their dreams. Through these they will become godless and fearful, for they have worked all their work in a lie, and have worshiped stone. Therefore they will die in an instant."

"In those days, blessed are all they who accept the words of wisdom and understand them and observe the paths of the Highest, and walk in the path of his righteousness, and did not become godless with the godless. For they will be saved. Woe to you who spread evil to your neighbors, for you will be slain in Sheol. Woe to you who make deceitful and false measures, and who cause bitterness on the Earth. For they will thereby be completely consumed."

"Woe to you who build your houses through the terrible struggle of others, and all their building materials are the bricks and stones of sin. I tell you, you will have no peace. Woe to them who reject the measure and eternal heritage of their fathers and whose minds follow after idols, for they will have no rest. Woe to them who work unrighteousness and help oppression, and slay their neighbors until the day of the great judgment. For he will tear down your glory, and bring affliction on your hearts, and will arouse his fierce indignation, and destroy you all with the sword. All the holy and righteous will remember your sins."

Letter of Enoch - Chapter 10

[ENOCH CONTINUED,] "IN those days, fathers and their sons will be destroyed together, and brothers with one another will fall in death until the streams flow with their blood. A man will not hold back his hand from killing his sons and his grandsons, and the sinner will not withhold his hand from his honored brother. From dawn until sunset they will slay one another. The horse will walk in the blood of sinners up to its chest, and the chariot will be submerged completely."

"In those days, the watchers will descend into the secret places and gather together into one place all those who brought down sin and the Highest will rise on that day of judgment to execute great judgment among sinners. Overall the righteous and holy he will appoint guardians from among the holy watchers to guard them like the apple of his eye, until he destroys all wickedness and sin, and though the righteous sleep a long sleep, they have nothing to fear."

"The children of the Earth will see the wise remain safe, and will understand all the words of this book, and recognize that their riches will not be able to save them from the punishment of their sins. Woe to you, sinners, on the day of your terrible punishment, you, who afflict the righteous and burn them with fire. You will be repaid according to your works. Woe to you, you with an obstinate heart, who watch to devise wickedness. Why will fear come over you, and there will be none to help you? Woe to you, you sinners, on account of the words of your mouth, and on account of the deeds of your hands which your godlessness as worked, in blazing flames burning worse than fire will you burn!"

"Know that he will inquire about your deeds from the watchers in the sky, from the sun, the moon, and the stars about your sins, because on the Earth you make judgments against the righteous. He will summon every cloud, mist, dew, and rain to testify against you, for they will all be stopped from descending on you, and they will remember your sins. Make sacrifices to the rain that it is not stopped from descending on you, or the dew, and when it has received gold and silver from you that it may descend. When the hoar-frost and snow with their frigidness and all the snow-storms with all their plagues fall on you, in those days you will not be able to stand before them."

Letter of Enoch - Chapter 11

[ENOCH CONTINUED,] "WATCH the sky, you children of the sky, and every work of the Highest, and fear him and do no evil in his presence. If he closes the windows of the sky and withholds the rain and the dew from falling on the Earth on your account, what will you do then? If he sends his anger on you because of your deeds, you cannot petition him, for you spoke proud and insolent words against his righteousness, and therefore you will have no peace."

"Don't you see the sailors of the ships? How their ships are tossed to and fro by the waves, and are shaken by the winds, and are in terrible trouble? They are afraid because all their possessions go on the sea with them, and they have terrible forebodings in their hearts that the sea will swallow them and they will die. Is not the entire sea and all its waters, and all its movements, the work of the Highest, and has he not set limits to its doings, and confined it by the sand? At his command, it is afraid and dries up, and all its fish die and all that is in it, but you sinners that are on the Earth don't fear him. Has he not made the sky and the Earth, and all that is within it? Who has the wisdom to understand everything that moves on the Earth and in the sea? Do not the sailors of the ships fear the sea? Yet sinners don't fear the Highest!"

Letter of Enoch - Chapter 12

[ENOCH CONTINUED,] "IN those days when he has brought a terrible fire on you, where will you run, and where will you find deliverance? When he speaks out against you will, you not be terrified?"

"All the luminaries will be terrified, and the Earth will tremble in fear and be alarmed. All the watchers will execute their commands and will seek to hide themselves from the presence of the Great Glory, and the children of Earth will tremble and quake. You sinners will be cursed forever, and you will have no peace. Don't fear, you minds[L20] of the righteous, be hopeful you that die in righteousness. Don't grieve if your mind descends into Sheol in grief and if in your life your body was not repaid for your goodness, but wait for the day of the judgment of sinners and for the day of cursing and punishment."

"When you, die the sinners will say about you, 'As we die, so the righteous die, and what benefit do they reap for their deeds? Look, like us they die in grief and darkness, and what have they gained over us? From now on we are equal. What will they receive and what will they see forever? Look, they too have died, and from now on forever will they see no light.'"

"I tell you, you sinners, you are content to eat and drink, and rob and sin, and strip men naked, and acquire wealth and see good days. Have you seen the righteous how their end falls out, that no manner of violence is found in them till their death? Nevertheless, they perished and became as though they had not been, and their spirits descended into Sheol in tribulation."

Letter of Enoch - Chapter 13

[ENOCH CONTINUED,] "NOW, therefore, I swear to you, the righteous, in the glory of the great, honored, mighty one who rules, and by his greatness I swear to you, I know a secret and have read the heavenly tablets, and have seen the holy books, and have found written and inscribed on them. All goodness and joy and glory are prepared for them, and written down for the spirits of those who have died in righteousness, and that a great deal of good will be given to you in repayment for your labors, and that your lot is great beyond the lot of the living."

"The spirits of you who have died in righteousness will live and rejoice, and their spirits will not die, or their memorial from before the face of the great one to all the generations of the world, therefore, don't fear them being abused."

"Woe to you, you sinners, when you have died, if you die in the wealth of your sins, and those who are like you say regarding you, 'Blessed are the sinners. They have seen all their days. How they have died in prosperity and wealth, and have not seen tribulation or murder in their life. They have died in honor, and judgment has not been executed on them during their life.'"

"Know that their minds will be made to descend into Sheol and they will be wretched in their great tribulation. Into darkness and chains and a burning flame where there is terrible judgment will your spirits enter. The great judgment will be for all the generations of the world. Woe to you, for you will have no peace."

"Don't say about the righteous and good who are alive, 'In our troubled days we have struggled laboriously and experienced every trouble, and met with much evil and been consumed, and have become few and our spirit small. We have been destroyed and have not found any to help us even with a word. We have been tortured and destroyed, and not hoped to see life from day to day. We hoped to be the head and have become the tail. We have struggled laboriously and had no satisfaction in our struggle. We have become the food of the sinners and the unrighteous, and they have laid their yoke heavily on us. They have had dominion over us that hated us and hit us. To those that hated us, we have bowed our necks but they pitied us not. We desired to get away from them that we might escape and be at rest but found no place where we should flee and be safe from them. Are complained to the rulers in our tribulation, and cried out against those who devoured us, but they did not listen to our cries and would not hear our voice. They helped those who robbed us and devoured us and those who made us few. They concealed their oppression, and they did not remove from us the yoke of those that devoured us and dispersed us and murdered us, and they concealed their murder, and remembered not that they had lifted their hands against us.'"

Letter of Enoch - Chapter 14

[ENOCH CONTINUED,] "I swear to you, that in the sky the watchers will remember you as good before the glory of the great one, and your names will be written before the glory of the great one. Be hopeful, for previously you were put to shame through affliction, but now you will shine like the lights of the sky, you will shine and you will be seen, and the portals of the sky will be opened to you. In your prayer, pray for judgment and it will appear for you, as all your tribulation will be visited on the rulers, and on all who helped those who plundered you. Be hopeful, and don't abandon your hopes for you will have great joy like the watchers of the sky. What will you be obliged to do? You will not have to hide on the day of the great judgment and you will not be caught as sinners, and the eternal judgment will be far from you for all the generations of the world. Don't be afraid you righteous, when you see the sinners growing strong and prospering in their ways. Do not be companions with them, but keep far from their violence, for you will become companions of the armies of the sky."

"Although you sinners say, 'All our sins will not be found out and recorded,' nevertheless, they will write down all your sins every day. I tell you that light and darkness and day and night see all your sins! Do not be godless in your hearts. Don't lie and don't alter the words of the upright, or accuse the words of the holy great one of lying, or have faith in your idols, for all your lying and all your godlessness do not come from righteousness but great sin."

"Now I know this mystery, that sinners will alter and pervert the words of righteousness in many ways, and will speak wicked words, and lie, and practice great deceits, and write books concerning their words. But when they write down truthfully all my words in their languages, and do not change or alter from my words but write them all down truthfully, all that I first testified concerning them, then I know another mystery, that books will be given to the righteous and the wise to become a cause of joy and uprightness and much wisdom. To them, the books will be given, and they will believe in them and rejoice over them, and then will all the righteous who have learned the paths of uprightness from them be repaid."

Letter of Enoch - Chapter 15

[ENOCH CONTINUED,] "IN those days the Lord commanded them to summon and testify to the children of Earth concerning their wisdom, saying, 'Show it to them, for you are their guides and a recompense over the whole Earth. For me and my son will be united with them forever in the paths of uprightness in their lives, and you will have peace. Rejoice, you children of uprightness. Amen.'"

Letter of Enoch - Chapter 16

[ENOCH CONTINUED,] "AFTER some days my son Methuselah took a wife for his son Lamech, and she became pregnant by him and carried a son. His body was white as snow and red as the blooming of a rose. The hair on his head was long locks as white as wool, and his eyes beautiful. When he opened his eyes, he lit up the whole house like the sun, and the whole house was very bright. He rose in the hands of the midwife, opened his mouth, and spoke with the Lord of righteousness."

"He, [Lamech,] said to him, [Methuselah,] 'I have begotten a strange son, completely unlike man, and resembling the sons of the sky god, and his nature is different and he is not like us. His eyes are like the rays of the sun, and his appearance is glorious.'"

"He, [Lamech] said to him, [Methuselah,] 'I have fathered a strange son, different from us and unlike man, and resembling the sons of the sky god! His nature is different and he is not like us, and his eyes are like the rays of the sun, and his countenance is glorious. It seems to me that he has not sprung from me but the watchers, and I fear that in his days a wonder may be worked on the Earth. Now, my father, I am here to petition you and implore you that you may go to Enoch, our fore-father, and learn from him the truth, as he lives among the watchers.'"

"When Methuselah heard the words of his son, he came to me at the edge of the Earth, for he had heard that I was there, and he called out, and I heard his voice and went to him, and said, 'Look, I am here my son, why have you come to me?'"

"He answered, 'I have come to you because of a great cause of anxiety, and because of a disturbing sight have I approached. Now, my father, hear me. To Lamech my son, there has been born a son, the like of whom there is none. His nature is not like man's nature, and the color of his body is whiter than snow and redder than the bloom of a rose, and the hair of his head is whiter than white wool, and his eyes are like the rays of the sun, and he opened his eyes and they lit up the whole house. He arose in the hands of the midwife, and opened his mouth and blessed the Lord of the sky. His father Lamech became afraid and fled to me, and did not believe that he was sprung from him, but that he was in the likeness of the watchers of the sky. I have come to you that you may tell me the truth.'"

"I, Enoch, answered, 'The Lord will do something new on the Earth. I have already seen this in a vision, and now tell you that in the generation of my father Jared some of the watchers of the sky transgressed the word of the Lord. They commit sin and transgress the law, and have united themselves with women and commit sin with them, and have married some of them, and have fathered children by them. They will produce on the Earth giants, not of the spirit, but the flesh, and there will be a great punishment on the Earth, and the Earth will be cleansed from all impurity. Yes, there will come a great destruction over the whole Earth, and there will be a deluge and a great destruction for one year. This son who has been born to you will be left on the Earth, and his three children will be saved with him. When all mankind that is on the Earth dies, he and his sons will be saved. Now tell your son Lamech that he who has been born is in truth his son, and call his name Noah, for he will be left from you, and he and his sons will be saved from the destruction, which will come on the Earth on account of all the sin and all the unrighteousness, which will be consummated on the Earth in his days. After that, there will be still more unrighteousness than that which was first committed on the Earth, for I know the secrets of the holy ones, and the Lord, has shown me and informed me, and I have read the heavenly tablets.'"

Letter of Enoch - Chapter 17

[ENOCH CONTINUED,] "I saw written on them that generation after generation will transgress until a generation of righteousness arises, and transgression is destroyed and sin passes away from the Earth, and all manner of good comes on it. Now, my son, go and tell your son Lamech that this son, which has been born, is in truth his son, and it is no lie."

"When Methuselah had heard the words of his father Enoch, and he showed to him everything in secret, he returned and told him and called the name of that son Noah, for he will comfort the Earth after all the destruction."

Letter of Enoch - Chapter 18

ANOTHER BOOK THAT ENOCH wrote for his son Methuselah and for those who will come after him, and follow the law in the last days.

You who have done good will wait for those days until an end of those who work evil comes, and the mighty transgressor end. Wait until sin has passed away, for their names will be blotted out of the book of life and out of the holy books, and their seed will be destroyed forever, and their spirits will be slain, and they will cry and make lamentation in a place that is a chaotic wilderness, and in the fire will they burn, for there is no Earth there. I saw there something like an invisible cloud, as because of its depth I could see over it, and I saw a flame of fire blazing brightly, and things like shining mountains circling and sweeping around. I asked one of the holy watchers who was with me, "What is this shining thing? It is not the sky but only the flame of a blazing fire, and the voice of weeping and crying and lamentation and strong pain."

He said to me, "Into this place you see here thrown the spirits of sinners and blasphemers, and of those who work wickedness, and of those who pervert everything that the Lord has spoken from the mouth of the prophets, predictions things have yet to come. Some of them are written and inscribed above in the sky, so the watchers may read them and know what will befall the sinners, and the spirits of the humiliated, and of those who have punished their bodies, and been recompensed by God, and of those who have been put to shame by wicked men, and who love God and loved neither gold, nor silver, nor any of the good things which are in the world, but gave over their bodies to torture. Who, since they came into being, did not long for earthly food, but regarded everything as a passing breath, and lived accordingly, and the Lord tested them much, and their spirits were found pure so that they should bless his name. All the blessings destined for them I have recounted in the books."

"He has assigned them their repayment, because they have been found to have loved the Sky more than their life in the world, and though they were trodden under foot of wicked men, and experienced abuse and insults and were put to shame, yet they blessed me. Now I will summon the spirits of the good who belong to the generation of light, and I will transform those who were born in darkness, who in the flesh were not recompensed with such honor as their faithfulness deserved. I will bring our in shining light those who have loved my holy name, and I will seat each on the throne of his honor. They will be resplendent for times without number, for righteousness is the judgment of God, for to the faithful he will give faithfulness in the habitation of upright paths. They will see those who were, born in darkness led into darkness, while the righteous will be resplendent. The sinners will cry aloud and see them resplendent, and they indeed will go where days and seasons are prescribed for them."

Book of the Watchers Notes

W1 The various translations of the Book of the Watchers that survive to the present all use the term 'holy one' or 'holy ones.' The term Holy One is the direct translation of the Canaanite 'Qadeshtu,' meaning the original text was likely written in Canaanite.

W2 The Holy One in the Sky was the title of Asherah in the early Israelite religion. Asherah was the name of an Israelite goddess before the time of Elijah in the 9th century, described as either the mother or wife of Yahweh, as well as the wife of El or Ba'al. By the 5th century, she had been replaced by the Canaanite war goddess Anat as the wife of Yahweh. It is unclear exactly how Asherah was worshiped, however the groves mentioned in the Torah and later Jewish texts are believed to be connected with her worship.

W3 Aramaic: 'rn (עירין). Translation: watcher, watchman, sentinel, guardian.

This word appears a number of times in the text and has been recovered within the fragments of Enoch found in the Dead Sea Scrolls. It was transliterated as Grigori in

W4 Aramaic: v'l (בעל). Generally transliterated as Baal or Ba'al. Translation: owner, lord, master, or husband.

Ge'ez: bal (??)

Ba'al was the Canaanite and later Hebrew and Aramaic term which translates as 'the Lord.' If the text is of Canaanite origin, then the Lord in the text was likely Ba'al Hadad, the 'Lord of Thunder' in the Canaanite pantheon.

W5 Aramaic: shmchzh (שמיחזה)

Greek: Semiaza (Σεμιαζά)

Samyaza is also transliterated as Sahjaza, Semihazah, Shemihazah, Shemyazaz, Shemyaza, Shemhazai, Sêmîazâz, Semjâzâ, Samjâzâ, and Semyaza. The definition of this name is unclear, however, within Rabbinical tradition, it is interpreted as either 'the name (God) has seen' or 'I have seen.'

The name itself is similar to the name of Canaanite and Akkadian god Shamash, the sun god. Shamash was the Akkadian version of the Sumerian god Utu, the twin brother of Inanna, who was the precursor to the Canaanite and Israelite goddess

Asherah, indicating that the origin of the Enoch story was likely in the Canaanite era, or, during the dark age that followed the Bronze Age collapse.

W6 Mount Hermon is a prominent mountain in the Anti-Lebanon mountains in northern modern Israel, southwest Syria, and southeast Lebanon, with a UN Buffer Zone between them. Mount Hermon was not generally important within Judaism, and only mentioned as a geographic location in the older sections of the Tanakh (Christian Old Testament), specifically in the books of Deuteronomy, Joshua, Judges, Dibra Hayyamim (Orthodox: 1st Paralipomenon, Catholic: 1st Chronicles), Psalms, and the Song of Songs (Catholic: Song of Solomon). In the Ugaritic Texts, from circa 1300 BC, Mount Herman was reported as being the home of Ba'al.

W7 Danel translates in Canaanite as 'El (God) is the Judge.' There was a Canaanite cultural hero named Danel the father of Aqhat recorded in the Epic of Aqhat from circa 1300 BC.

W8 Three thousand cubits would make these giants 1.62 km (1 mile) tall.

W9 Hebrew: 'ammoh (אַמָּה). Translation: cubits

The length of the cubit changed from culture to culture and through time. Around the time the Septuagint was translated into Greek, the Greek cubit was approximately 46 cm (18 inches), while the Judean cubit is believed to have been around 51 cm (21 inches).

W10 Hebrew: 'eretz (אֶרֶץ). Translations: land, earth, ground, Earth, country, soil

The Earth / Ge is depicted as the same type of primordial deity in the Septuagint as it was in the Greek myths, and called on to witness blessings and curses, implying consciousness.

W11 Hebrew: nefesh (נֶפֶשׁ). Translation: mind, life, soul, person

Greek: psychên (ψυχήν). Translation: mind, personality, psyche

This is generally used only in relation to humans and angels who have a more developed mind.

W12 Greek: ypsístou (ὑψίστου)

The Highest is a reference to God, or a god, found in many ancient religions in the region. According to the Torah, the ancient people of Jerusalem worshiped El Elyon, which translates as 'Highest God' when Abraham passed through the regions. The term Highest repeats though other early Jewish and Samaritan texts. In the Septuagint's Torah, the Highest was the God above Iaw (Yahweh).

W13 Hebrew: dvdl (דודאל). Generally transliterated as Dudael from דּוּדָאֵל

Dudael is a name composed of the terms 'dvd' (דוד) meaning cauldron or kettle, and 'l' (אל) meaning god, God, or El (the supreme Canaanite god). Therefore Dudael translates as approximately Cauldron of God (or El). In the Greco-Roman era it was considered the equivalent of Hades. Its entrance was said to be somewhere east of Jerusalem.

This term is extremely rare, and is one of the reasons that we theorized that the Book of the Watchers might have been written in Hebrew or Aramaic before finding the Dead Sea Scrolls.

W14 Hebrew: tehom (תהום). Translations: deep, depths, deep sea, subterranean waters, grave

Greek: abyssos (ἀβύσσου). Translation: abyss, another name for Tartarus - the Greek primordial underworld god

The abyss is a common element in most ancient mid-east religions. It was imagined as an infinitely deep dark place, generally filled with fresh water. The Akkadians and Babylonians called in tamtu, and in Ugaritic Canaanite it was t-h-m. Both terms and the later Hebrew tehom are believed to derive from the Sumerian name Tiamat, who was a goddess that lived in the depths of the ocean. The Sumerian term for the abyss was Abzu, which is likely where the Greek term abyssos ultimately derives from. In Egyptian beliefs, the abyss was called Nu, and like many of the other religion this sea was seen as being both below the Earth, and above Sky, and reaching off to infinity. All of these concepts seem to be an early attempt to envision what is now called outer space.

W15 Ge'ez: Ublesjael

Aramaic: Abelsjail

The location of meadow of waters has been debated for centuries. Many believe it is a corruption of Abel-maim, from the ancient Jewish book of Kings (Christian 1st Kings/Kingdoms), however, the location of Abel-maim is also unknown and debated. In Canaanite, Abel-maim meant 'Meadow of waters,' however later in Hebrew Abel-maim meant 'Mourning of waters.'

Currently the dominant view is that Abel-maim may have been the ruins of Tell Abil el-Qameḥ, located on the northern border of modern Israel, about 2 km south of the town of Metula and about 6.5 km west of Tel Dan. Nothing has been found at the site that connects it to Abel-maim (or meadow of waters), and it is identified as being Abel-maim simply because of the described geography of the site in the book of Kings.

The settlement at Tell Abil el-Qameḥ existed from at least the late bronze-age into the early iron-age. Artifacts from the site have been dated back to at least 1300 BC, and the town appears to have existed until the Assyrians conquered Samaria. It was reoccupied during the Persian era, and continued to be occupied until the Ottoman Empire. Some archaeologists believe Tell Abil el-Qameḥ was mentioned in the Execration Texts from Pharaoh Thutmose III, as well as the Amarna Letters, meaning the town had to have been significant by the 1450s BC.

Based on the location of meadow of waters within this text, between the mountains of Lebanon and Mount Hermon (Sirion) in the Anti-Lebanon mountains, it was likely of the Jordan River, and could have been Tell Abil el-Qameḥ or Abel-maim, and therefore the translation 'Meadow of waters' is used in this translation.

W16 Ge'ez: Seneser

Canaanite: Sirion

This is the ancient Canaanite name for Mount Hermon. It later became the Hebrew word for breastplate. Sirion is the name of Hermon in the Bronze Age Ugaritic poem about Baal and Anath. Ugarit was a city on the Mediterranean coast of ancient Canaan, on the modern Syrian coast, which existed between 6000 and 1190 BC. In 1929 AD, an archive of ancient Canaanite texts was discovered there, now know collectively as the Ugaritic Texts.

The fact that the Canaanite word was used implies that some of the text the Book of the Watchers may date back to bronze-age Canaan. It is certainly set in bronze-age Canaan.

W17 Hebrew: chrvv (כרוב). Generally transliterated as Cherub

Cherubs were widely depicted in Canaanite art, however, it is unclear what their origin was. Some of the surviving early cherubs found in ancient Canaanite ruins at Megiddo dating to 1300 to 1200 BC look sphinx-like, implying an Egyptian origin. The depictions of Cherubs from the Second Temple era looked more like the traditional depiction of angels, which is believed to have been adopted from the Assyrians during the Assyrian and Babylonian eras.

W18 Jacinth is an orange-red transparent variety of zircon used as a gemstone, that was widely traded in the ancient world.

W19 The seven stars trapped as the eastern edge of the world, appears to be a reference to the Pleiades star cluster, when they were the morning stars circa 2200 to 2000 BC. A similar reference to the Pleiades as the morning stars appears in the Book of Job. Ancient Egyptian sources also mention a Canaanite chieftain named Job from around 2000 BC, which seems to confirm the original story of Job was from around that time. This reference to the Pleiades as the morning stars, indicates the origin of the story of Enoch was from around the same time.

W20 If the origin of this paragraph is dated to circa 2200 to 2000 BC, then the end of the world would be dated to circa 7700 to 8000 AD. This time-frame is not consistent with late-Messianic-Judaism and early-Christianity, which both placed the end of the world circa 500 AD, or with Zoroastrianism, which had the cycle of destruction in 6000 year time-spans. The destruction of the world in 500 AD, 6000 AM using the history of the world found in the Septuagint, is theorized to have been imported to Messianic-Judaism from Zoroastrianism during the Persian rule of Judea, circa 525 to 330 BC, which means this text must be older than that, given the time-frame points to a longer than 10,000 year cycle of destruction.

W21 Ge'ez: Sis (??). Translation: Siren (likely derived from the Greek concept)

Aramaic equivalent: tzfr (צפרא). Translation: morning

Greek term in the Septuagint: Sirên (Σειρήν)

Siren is a Greek term, however, also appears in the Septuagint, in the book of Isiah and Jeremiah. In the Masoretic texts, the term used in Isaiah is 'jackals' while in Jeremiah it is 'owls.' The fact that Sirens (??) is used in Ge'ez, implies that the Ge'ez translation was ultimately derived from a Greek translation, or, from an Aramaic source.

The Greek term 'Siren,' like much of Greek mythology, was originally derived from a Canaanite term, in this case the word for 'female singer,' and therefore if the Book of the Watchers did date back to the Canaanite era, the Canaanite author likely meant 'female singers,' likely in in the same way the Greeks used the word 'Sirens.' As the books of Isaiah and Jeremiah would have also have been written in Canaanite (Paleo-Hebrew), the Canaanite term for 'female-singer' was likely used in the original texts as well.

W22 Greek: Τάρταρος (Tartaros). Translation: underworld

In Greek mythology, Tartarus was a location in the Abyss, like Hades. The term Tartarus is an anachronism in the Book of the Watchers, and was once used to date the book to the Greek era, however, since the discovery of the Dead Sea scrolls it is clear the book was written earlier. The original term was likely Mirey (hmry), the Canaanite term for 'pit,' which was used in a similar way to the Greek term Tartarus.

W23 Greek: χάος (chaos).

In Greek mythology, Chaos was a term used to describe the theoretical concept of the vast void that existed before the world. The term chaos is an anachronism in the Book of the Watchers, and was once used to date the book to the Greek era, however, since the discovery of the Dead Sea scrolls it is clear the book was written earlier. A similar concept was described in the Torah as Tohu wa-bohu (תהו ובהו) which indicates a similar concept was known in the early Israelite religion, and likely the Canaanite religion at the time.

W24 Aramaic: pardaysa (פרדס). Translation: royal park

Greek: paradison (παράδεισον). Translation: paradise, garden with a wall around it

The word paradise is ultimately derived from the Zoroastrian religion holy book the Avesta. The Avestan word was pairi-daêza (??????????), which translated as 'walled enclosure.' By the 6th century BC the word had been adopted by the Assyrians, and was subsequently adopted by the Samaritans and other peoples conquered by the Assyrians.

The term paradise is an anachronism in the Book of the Watchers, and could be used to date the book to the Persian era, however, the term could also have entered into the Canaanite religion earlier, as there were Indo-Iranians in the Mitanni Empire in the territory of Syria circa 1500 to 1300 BC, as well as in the Habiru marauders between 1800 and 1200 BC.

W25 Ge'ez: akyəst (?????). Translation: dragon, serpent

Hebrew: srf (שׂרף). Generally transliteration: seraph

Greek: seraphim (σεραφείμ)

The Hebrew term was a continuation of the Canaanite word for 'snake,' however, does not appear to have been used in Hebrew to mean 'snake.' The seraph appears to have been imported into the Canaanite religion from Egypt during the Hyksos era, and is believed by historians to have originated in the Egyptian uraeus. The uraeus was the stylized Egyptian cobra in the crown of pharaoh which represented the goddess Wadjet, the serpent goddess of ancient Egypt who was worshiped since pre-dynastic times.

W26 The middle of the Earth refers to the geographic center of the flat Earth, not the center of the spherical Earth. In early and medieval Christianity, Golgotha in Jerusalem was seen as the center of the flat Earth. This text is clearly not describing Jerusalem, which indicates the text is pre-Second Temple era, and likely before Solomon's Temple as well.

W27 Mastic is a plant that grows in Arabia that has been used to produce resin since ancient times. It is also called Arabic gum, Yemen gum, or tears of Chios in Greece, as is was also produced on the Greek island of Chios.

W28 Galbanum is plant indigenous to the territory of modern Iran which produces an aromatic gum resin that was widely traded in the ancient world. In Greek mythology, when Prometheus stole fire from the gods and gave it to humanity, he gave it in the form of a torch burning galbanum gum. It was also used in medicine in the classical era, and continues to be used in medicine to this day.

W29 Stacte was the name of a component of the incense described in the Exodus. It is not clear what exactly it was, however, is generally accepted as a product of myrrh. It is also sometimes though to be storax, cinnamon oil, or a number of other things.

W30 The watcher Zotiel is a unique term, found only once in the five Books of Enoch. It is also not found in the Secrets of Enoch, the Revelation of Metatron, or any other surviving ancient Hebrew or Canaanite texts.

The 'watcher Zotiel' may to be related to the Zoroastrian Hara Berezaiti which translates as 'high watchpost' in the Avestan language, which is the mythical mountain at the north-pole around which all the stars circle. It is plausible that Hara Berezaiti started as an Avestan interpretation of Thuban (Alpha Draconis) which was the north star between 3900 and 1800 BC, or Tau Herculis which was the north star circa 7400 BC. If the watcher Zotiel is based in Hara Berezaiti, then then this section of the Book of the Watchers likely dates to the Persian era, however, it could be a relic from an earlier period, as there were Indo-Iranians in the Mitanni Empire in the territory of Syria circa 1500 to 1300 BC, as well as in the Habiru marauders between 1800 and 1200 BC.

W31 The setting in which Enoch was apparently writing this text was in southern Lebanon, which was the major lumber source for ancient Egypt.

W32 Hebrew: mlch hchvvd (מלך הכבוד) often transliterated as Melek Hakavod. Translation: King of Glory (or Honor, Justice).

Ba'al Hakavod is a term that also shows up in the later books of Enoch. 'Melek Hakavod' means 'King of Glory (or Honor, Justice)' or possibly 'the Glorious (or

Honorable, Just) Moloch,' as both melek and Moloch are spelled the same in Hebrew (מלך).

Book of Parables Notes

P1 The term 'holy one' indicates a Hebrew or Aramaic source for the surviving Ge'ez translation, which would have used the term kdosh (קדש) which translates as 'holy' or 'sacred.' This word is used in the Masoretic Texts and was translated in the Septuagint as hagios (ἅγιος), which is generally translated by the English-speaking Christians as 'saint,' from the Latin term sanctus, which was a title for people that worked at the temples in the old Roman cults.

The term 'Holy One of the Sky' is used throughout the 1st Book of Enoch, the Book of the Watchers, which appears to be Canaanite in origin. The Holy One in the Sky was the title of Asherah in the Canaanite and early Israelite religions. Asherah was the name of an Israelite goddess before the time of Elijah in the 9th century, described as either the mother or wife of Yahweh (Iaw), as well as the wife of El or Ba'al. By the 5th century, she had been replaced by the Canaanite war goddess Anat as the wife of Yahweh. It is unclear exactly how Asherah was worshiped, however, the groves mentioned in the Torah and later Jewish texts are believed to be connected with her worship.

The Book of Parables does not appear to be making reference to Asherah and uses the term 'holy one' similar to the way the Hebrew text use the term kdosh (קדש), which implied the Hebrew or Aramaic copy was composed under Persian influence or later.

In this opening verse, Enoch seems to be referring to himself as the 'Holy One,' however, this title does not seem to always apply to him. The inconsistent use of 'holy one' appears related to the conflicting viewpoint in later chapters which switch abruptly between the viewpoint of Enoch and Noah. This implies that the entire Book of Parables may have been cut from a book about Noah, like the Book of Giants, which was similar to the books of Enoch.

P2 The term Lord of Spirit is an unusual term, that is not found in the other books of Enoch, and is not found in other ancient Jewish Texts.

The term may be a translation of the Akkadian (Babylonian and Assyrian) Ellil, which is composed of the Akkadian word El and Lil. In Akkadian El meant 'lord,' 'leader,' or figuratively 'god,' while 'lil' translated as 'wind,' 'breath,' 'spirit,' 'ghost,' or 'phantom.'

In the Akkadian (originally Sumerian, later Babylonian and Assyrian) story of the great flood, the god that caused the flood was Enlil (Sumerian Enlil), while the god Ea (Sumerian Enki) tried to save humanity by warning the Noah character that it was coming. See the note on the Head of Days for more information on the Mesopotamian Noah character. This story of the great flood is paralleled in the Book of Parables, however, it is caused by the 'Head of Days,' not the 'Lord of Spirit,' meaning that while there are similar characters, the roles have been changed.

By the Neo-Babylonian era, Ellil was no longer being worshiped as a god, having been replaced by Bel, who shows up in the Septuagint's version of the book of Daniel. Bel translates as 'Lord', and could be the Lord referred to in the book of Parables. In the Neo-Babylonian era, Bel had replaced several older gods, taking on the roles of Ellil, Marduk, and Dumuzid, which implies the original Akkadian version source text for the Book of Parables was older than the Neo-Babylonian era. Ellil was replaced by the god Marduk, the national god of Babylon, during the Old Babylonian empire, implying the Babylonian source text used for some sections of the Book of Parables was an Akkadian text, likely written before 1500 BC.

P3 Hebrew: glgl (גלגל), generally transliterated as galgal. Translation: wheel, sphere, whirlwind.

The term 'galgal' is generally translated as 'whirlwind' or 'circle within circle.' People were sometimes described as traveling via whirlwind to the sky or the moon in ancient Greco-Roman literature, such as Lucian's *True History*, and therefore it is plausible that the term glgl did mean whirlwind, however, the connotation is the same as vfn (אופן).

P4 The term 'Satans' is plural in the Book of Parables, as well in the Secrets of Enoch. The Secrets of Enoch names them as Yeqon, Asbeel, Gadreel, Penemue, and Kasdaye, all of which are listed as watchers in the Book of Parables, implying that the Secrets of Enoch is dependent on the Book of Parables, or both are dependent on a common earlier source-text. In Hebrew, the word stn (שׂטן) meant accuser or contender, and was not generally viewed as being a single being, but any who questioned God.

P5 All the cultures in the Middle East had a masculine solar deity. The Akkadians, Babylonians, Assyrians Canaanites, and Arameans worshiped Shemesh (Shamash or Shapash), who is mentioned in the early Israelite texts. The Egyptians worshiped Atum and Ra, who Moses likely worshiped. The Sumerians worshiped Utu. The Greeks worshiped Helios and later Apollo, and the early Persians worshiped Hvarekhshaeta who the 6th Yasht in the Avesta is dedicated to.

P6 Hebrew: Yarikh (ירח). Definition: the moon, Yarikh (the Canaanite lunar god)

Yarikh was a Canaanite and Arabian god, also called Ya Rehuhm by the Sabean Arabs, Ya Rekuhn by the Mofarite Arabs, and Ya Rekan by the Ge'ez speaking Ethiopians. Yarikh was not described as being feminine, but masculine like the other Semitic Lunar gods.

The relationship between the Lord (Ba'al), moon, and sun described in the text, is similar to the Trinity of Aramaic gods: Bel, Yarikh, and Yarhibol, who were worshiped in Palmyra before the worship of the Bel Marduk replaced them in the early-1st-millennium, implying the original text may date back to that time. However, Yarikh was not depicted as a goddess, but rather a god by the ancient Arameans, which implies the text was updated during the Persian or Greek eras, as both cultures saw the sun as masculine and the moon as feminine. The Persians viewed the moon as the goddess Mah (Avestan Manha, Old Persian Maha), and the sun as god Hvarekhshaeta, while the Greeks depicted the sun as the masculine Titan Helios, and later the god Apollo, and the moon as the feminine Titan Selene and later the goddess Artemis. The genders were most likely applied to the text during the translation to Hebrew from Canaanite (Paleo-Hebrew) sometime between 539 and 200 BC, as the Books of Enoch virtually disappeared by that time.

It is also believed by some scholars that Asherah may have been interpreted as a Lunar goddess, based on the crescent in her crown, however, the dominant view is that it was not a crescent, but horns.

P7 Wisdom is also a goddess or spirit of some kind in the Hebrew book of Proverbs, which is traditionally attributed to Solomon, however, is now known to be a compilation of Proverbs, some of which were copied from the much older Wisdom of Amenenope. In the Hebrew texts, the word chchmvs (חכמות) is used, which is often described as a 'feminine plural indefinite form' of chchm (חכם), meaning 'sage,' 'wisdom,' or 'clever.' The Greeks at the Library of Alexandria translated the Hebrew term chchmvs (חכמות) as Sophia (Σοφία) meaning wisdom and treated her as a type of spirit or god within the text. She was later adopted by the Gnostics of the 2nd-century AD, where she was sometimes described as the wife of God, or the wife of Jesus, or an Aeon which was a type of lesser god.

The nature of the Hebrew term has been debated for thousands of years and could have stated as a reference to the Priestess of Chmvsh (כמוש), more commonly known as the Moabite god as Chemosh. He is recorded in a number of ancient Canaanite and Israelite documents including the Mesha Stele from circa 840 BC, various Elbite tablets from between 3500 and 700 BC. According to the 3rd Kingdoms chapter 11, King Solomon built a Temple to Chemosh on the Mount of Olives, which according to 4th Kingdoms chapter 23, was later torn down by King Josiah when he instituted his 'one god policy.' As the term used here denotes a sentient being, the

Greek Sophia is used in the translation, although 'Priestess of Chemosh' might be more appropriate if translating from the Hebrew.

The use of Sophia (Σοφία) as a translation for chchmvs (חכמות) was already present in the Septuagint's book of Proverbs by 132 BC, and therefore was not something that originated with the Christians or Gnostics. In Proverbs, she was depicted similarly to the way she is depicted in the Book of Parables. It is likely that this section of the book dates to the Greek era, between 330 and 150 BC, however, could also have originated in the Persian era under the influence of the Persian goddess Anahita, who was also a wisdom-goddess, or much earlier in the Canaanite era under the influence of the Egyptian goddess Seshat, the goddess of wisdom, knowledge, and writing.

P8 The Head of Days is often considered to be a scribal error in the Ge'ez translation, and that the original Aramaic text would have used the term 'Ancient of Days' which is also found in the Book of Daniel. As both texts fall into the messianic and prophet movements within Judaism, and both texts are likely Greek-era redactions of ancient Canaanite (Paleo-Hebrew) or Akkadian (Babylonian or Assyrian) texts, it is likely that the 'Head of Days' and 'Ancient of Days' share a common origin, however, it isn't possible to know which phrase is the more accurate translation of the original term in the Canaanite or Akkadian text.

Based on the fact that the story is clearly a parallel to the Mesopotamian flood narratives, and the likely pre-Persian origin of the text indicated by the references to Abzu and Tiamat in chapter 18, the similarity of the terms 'Head of Days,' and 'Ancient of Days' to Ziusudra and Utnapishtim should not be ignored. In the Mesopotamian flood stories, the Noah character had several different names depending on the culture and era, including Ziusudra and Utnapishtim both of which translated as something like 'life of long days' or 'finder of long days' in Sumerian and Akkadian respectively. He was also called Atra-Hasis which translates as 'extremely wise' in Akkadian. The name Atra-Hasis was also found on the Sumerian king list as the last king before the great flood, implying that Atra-Hasis is the older name and that Ziusudra and Utnapishtim were epithets or titles. During the Neo-Assyrian and Neo-Babylonian eras, the Akkadian term Utnapishtim was in common use within the Babylonian flood stories, meaning that 'Head of Days' and 'Ancient of Days' could both be attempts to translate 'Utnapishtim' into Hebrew.

As Utnapishtim was the Noah character in the Babylonian flood story, the Book of Parables is clearly not a direct translation of any known surviving version of the older Mesopotamian flood narratives, nevertheless, the latest this book is likely to have been written would have been during the Babylonian era, however, it could have originated significantly earlier as an alternative version of the flood narrative that the Hebrews for some reason adopted.

In the closing chapter of the Book of Parables, the Head of Days is referred to as 'that Head of Days,' implying this was a title, and there was more than one. This appears to parallel the Noah character in the Hindu religion, Manu, whose name means 'man' or 'human' like Adam. In the Sanskrit text the Manusmriti, Manu was the survivor of a flood along with other people he saved in his boat. The term Manu is used as a title, as he is the father of the new race of humans after the flood, and it is a title many Manus have held in the cycles of destruction and rebuilding according to the Manusmriti. This text is considered to be a composite of ancient texts standards into its current version during the Greek-era, circa 200 BC. The archaic language found in some sections of the Manusmriti have led some linguists to claim that the older sections could not date to between 1250 and 1000 BC, and the text is believed to have circulated within the Persian empire, like the other Sanskrit texts of the time. An influence of the Manusmriti on the Book of Parables cannot be proven from one word, but the two texts are both about great floods that destroyed ancient worlds and the progenitors of new generations, which makes it likely the translators and editors of the Book of Parables would have at least studied the Manusmriti at some point.

P9 The term 'son of man' is often accepted as a reference to Jesus Christ by Christians, both modern Christians and early Christians, as it is similar to the title 'Son of Man' found in the Apocalypse of John, however, the term used in the Book of Parables always includes a qualifier such as 'this son of man' or 'that son of man,' implying that the Parables predate the Apocalypse of John, where 'Son of Man' is used as a proper title.

The description of the Son of Man is clearly not a description of Jesus Christ, as the son of man in the Parables of Enoch was depicted as a violent messianic figure, like the Jesus Christ in the Jewish Apocalypse of Ezra, which points to a Messianic Jewish group for this 'son of man' figure.

While Hebrew and Aramaic copies of the Book of Parables do not exist, if they did, the term 'son of man,' would have also translated as 'son of Adam,' which is likely what was meant here as Seth is mentioned in the opening line as the 'son of Adam.' The same term 'son of man' is used in other Babylonian era prophetic texts such as Ezekiel and Daniel, where it is translatable as either 'son of man' or 'son of Adam' from the Hebrew ben-'adam (בן־אדם).

According to the Torah, all humans are the children of Seth, however, there were at the time also another group of humans called the children of Cain. The third son of Adam named Abel had died before fathering any children. Therefore, as all non-

Cainite humans are the children of Seth, he is one who would return to the Earth to judge humanity other than the Cainites, who would be destroyed outright for the sins of Cain. In chapter 26 humans are referred to as the children of 'that son of man,' and therefore the term 'son of Adam' is used in their translation.

Seth was a character that was found in several ancient religions in the region, most famously in Egypt, where he became perceived as an evil-god by the New Kingdom era for apparently murdering his brother Osiris. He was the primary god worshiped by the Hyksos dynasty during their rule of Egypt and was vilified after the Egyptians drove them out, circa 1550 BC. In the Old Kingdom text, he was depicted as a heroic god who protected the sun-god Ra from the snake-dragon Apep. He was also the focus of the Sethite religion, whose texts were later adopted by the Gnostics in the early-Christian-era. The Sethites claimed that Seth had left Steles on the tops of some mountains that survived the great flood, from which they drew their theology. Another group reported to exist in the early-Christian era were the Cainites, however, these Cainites did not claim to be descendants of Cain, but rather named themselves after him as he was the first man killed by the 'evil creator.' These Cainites were a Gnostic sect that worshiped Sophia (Wisdom) and viewed the creator as an evil god. It is unclear when the Cainites originated, but all early-Christian scholars agreed that the Sethites were an ancient pre-Christian-era sect.

P10 Sheol (שאול) is the Hebrew term that translates ad grave. It was generally translated as Hades or Tartarus by the Greeks and is often mistranslated as Hell in English, even though it was never described as the pagan Germanic frozen wasteland of Hell. It was occasionally translated as being on fire, like Hades, as it is in the Book of Parables, however, it generally seems more symbolic of the concept of death.

P11 The reference to the masculine sky water, and feminine subterranean water, shows a clear Mesopotamian influence. In the Akkadian, Babylonian, and Assyrian religions, the world was created by the mixing of two primordial waters, Abzu and Tiamat. Abzu, also transliterated as Apsu, was the masculine primordial deity composed of the freshwater that was above the world. Tiamat was the feminine primordial deity composed of the salt-water that was below world, as the land was believed to float on a sea of salt-water.

The earliest surviving record of this creation story was found in the Old-Babylonian text called the Enuma Elish, which told the Old-Babylonian creation story. The text is believed to date to the Old-Babylonian Empire, circa 1900 BC, however, the Enuma Elish continued to be used throughout the history of the Assyrian and Babylonian cultures, and was still in use during the Neo-Assyrian and Neo-Babylonian Empires of the 7th and 6th centuries BC, meaning the Samaritans and Jews that were taken as captives would have been exposed to the Enuma Elish by that era. This is clearly a pre-Persian era reference, as both the Persians and later Greeks had not stories about the masculine sky-water mixing with the feminine subterranean-water.

P12 The reference to the coming destruction of the Medes and Persians dates this section of the text to the early Persian era but also indicates a pre-Ezra origin. It is unlikely that it was written earlier than the Persian-era, as the Persians were fairly unimportant in the affairs of Judea before they conquered the Babylonian Empire. The view of the Persians as an occupying force is the opposite view from the one recorded in the books of the scribe Ezra, who reported the Persians were the liberators of the Jews, although as he tried to convert the Jews to Zoroastrianism he may have been biased.

After he arrived in Jerusalem, the first thing he reported doing was kicking out the Samaritan priesthood, as well as the Jewish priests who could not prove their genealogy, from the temple they were building. It is plausible that this text was one being used by those priests, either Samaritan or one of the other Jewish sects Ezra kicked out. There is no evidence of the Books of Enoch ever being used by modern Samaritans, and in fact, it seems unlikely they did, as they used a version of the Torah, and the Torah and books of Enoch have some conflicts between them. If the Book of Parables was being used by some Jews in Jerusalem before Ezra arrived, that would mean a Hebrew form of the Book of Parables already existed by 457 BC.

P13 The flying chariots are found in many Jewish texts from the time of Ezekiel until about 1000 AD. Traditionally scholars assumed they were a Christian-era collection of works, but since the discovery of the dead sea scrolls, it is apparent that the chariots were common in pre-Christian-era Jewish works as well. These flying chariots were central to the Revelation of Metatron, which is a work of unknown origin focused on Enoch's life after he was taken up to heaven, that appears to have been written as a sequel to the Book of Parables, implying the Book of Parables and the Revelation of Metatron circulated together at one point separate from the other books of Enoch.

P14 The final destruction of darkness by Ahura Mazda (Lord of Wisdom), is a central theme of the Zoroastrian end of the world, which chapter 22 in the third parable seems to be paraphrasing. This chapter in the third parable seems to be a later insertion sometime during the Persian era, later than the second parable in which the Persians were an evil invading force. The rest of the third parable seems similar to the later books of Enoch, however, could not have originated in the same text as they are written from Noah's perspective, while the following books were written from Methuselah's perspective. This end-of-the-world description is repeated in the Persian-era Letter of Enoch, and the author of that Letter may have been the person that inserted this line, and possibly the person who unified the four older books with his letter.

P15 This sentence significantly diverges from the story of Enoch in the Torah, where Enoch only lived 365 years before God took him to paradise. It could be interpreted as something that happened after he was taken to paradise, however, it does not line up with the Torah's timeline for the flood of Noah either, which would have happened 1120 years after Enoch was born. This event would have happened 20 years before Noah was born using the chronology of the Masoretic Texts and Septuagint, or when Noah was 315 years old according to the Samaritan Torah. In all cases, the chronology does not correlate with any known version of the Torah, meaning the author was not using the Torah as a source document. The most likely explanation is that the parable in question was written by someone who did not have access to the Torah, however, this parable could have also originated as a translation of a story that was not originally about the Enoch from the Torah. The name in it could have been translated into a more familiar name with the rest of the text, especially if the author believed he had found an ancient text about Enoch.

P16 The Ge'ez text records the name as Duidain, however, this is believed to be a corruption of the wasteland of Dudael in the Book of the Watchers. Duidain is otherwise unknown in Hebrew or Aramaic texts.

Hebrew: dvdl (דודאל). Generally transliterated as Dudael from דּוּדָאֵל

Dudael is a name composed of the terms 'dvd' (דוד) meaning cauldron or kettle, and 'l' (אל) meaning god, God, or El (the supreme Canaanite god). Therefore Dudael translates as approximately Cauldron of God (or El). In the Greco-Roman era it was considered the equivalent of Hades. Its entrance was said to be somewhere east of Jerusalem.

This term is extremely rare, and is one of the reasons that we theorized that the Book of the Watchers might have been written in Hebrew or Aramaic before finding the Dead Sea Scrolls.

P17 This is a curious line that indicates the author of this parable was supposed to be Noah, and not Enoch. Enoch was the seventh from Adam, and Noah was his grandson. The internal implication is that the Book of Parables was a retelling by Noah after the flood. The text of this parable continues without clarifying whose viewpoint it is from, suggesting that this section of the parables was from a text by Noah that was merged with the text about Enoch at some point. The text suddenly switched back to Noah's perspective again in chapter 29.

P18 This chapter is missing what must be assumed to be a significant section of text about the Leviathan and Behemoth, otherwise found in the book of Job, which also ends abruptly while describing them, although a strange 'concluding chapter' where noting it resolved and Job 'wins the lottery' was tacked on to the end at some point. These two creatures were also mentioned in the Apocalypse of Ezra, which according to the Ethiopian Orthodox church was written by 'king of the exiles' Shealtiel in Babylon circa 567 BC. However, in the Apocalypse of Ezra, the author called Behemoth Enoch, implying that he did not have access to the Torah, book of Job, or books of Enoch. This is consistent with the history of the Torah found in the Babylonian Talmud, which claims the original Torah was stolen by the Assyrians, and Ezra later rewrote it from memory.

Little is known about these two creatures. In the book of Job, the Leviathan is described as some kind of steam-powered submarine, and the Behemoth sounds like a description of a dinosaur. According to various medieval Jewish texts, they were originally accompanied by a third creature called Aziz, who was some kind of flying monster.

The Leviathan is based on the older Canaanite Lotan, as some of the text in the book of Isaiah that describes the Leviathan repeats the ancient Canaanite Ugaritic texts almost verbatim, substituting the name Leviathan for Lotan. The Canaanite Lotan is also accepted as the source of the Greek myth of Ladon, the serpent-dragon that guarded the apple tree in the Garden of the Hesperides. Aziz the sky-monster is believed to have been based on the Canaanite god Ziz, the morning star, however, could equally be traced back to Anzu the enormous bird-like monster from Babylonian mythology, once called Imdugud by the Sumerians. It is unclear if there was a Canaanite predecessor to Behemoth, however, it is described similar to the monster named Humbaba in the Epic of Gilgamesh from circa 1800 BC. In the Epic of Gilgamesh, this monster was reported as living between the Lebanon and Anti-Lebanon mountain ranges, which is the same location that the Book of the Watchers describes the watchers living. Additionally, Humbaba is specifically called a 'Guardian,' which is the most common alternate translation of the Aramaic term iri (עִיר), which is herein translated as 'watcher.'

P19 Hebrew: chrvv (כרוב). Generally transliterated as Cherub

Cherubs were widely depicted in Canaanite art, however, it is unclear what their origin was. Some of the surviving early cherubs found in ancient Canaanite ruins at Megiddo dating to 1300 to 1200 BC look sphinx-like, implying an Egyptian origin. The depictions of Cherubs from the Second Temple era looked more like the traditional depiction of angels, which is believed to have been adopted from the Assyrians during the Assyrian and Babylonian eras.

P20 Ge'ez: akyəst (?????). Translation: dragon, serpent

Hebrew: srf (שׂרף). Generally transliteration: seraph

Greek: seraphim (σεραφείμ)

The Hebrew term was a continuation of the Canaanite word for 'snake,' however, does not appear to have been used in Hebrew to mean 'snake.' The seraph appears to have been imported into the Canaanite religion from Egypt during the Hyksos era, and is believed by historians to have originated in the Egyptian uraeus. The uraeus was the stylized Egyptian cobra in the crown of pharaoh which represented the goddess Wadjet, the serpent goddess of ancient Egypt who was worshiped since pre-dynastic times.

P21 Hebrew: vfn (אופן), generally transliterated as ophan. Translation: wheel.

Ophans are a strange and generally obscure term within modern Judaism, however, were a popular aspect of the Jewish Merkabah literature until around 1000 AD. Ophans are 'flying wheels,' generally described similar to the modern concept of a 'flying saucer,' however, considered to be working for God like the angels, and stars, clouds, and lightning. As the term ophan is not commonly found in English translations, the translation 'flying-wheel' is used in this text.

P22 Many of the gods throughout the Middle East, Eurasia, and Africa were depicted as having horns, including several Canaanite, Mesopotamian, and Egyptian deities. Many early priesthoods used horns in their head-gear, and some crowns have been found that included horns. In Egypt, the Hemhem crown was ceremonial headgear used by priests in ancient Egypt that included rams' horns during the New Kingdom era.

P23 In the Book of the Watchers this watcher was called Arakiel, some copies have Arakiba.

P24 In the Book of the Watchers this watcher was called Rameel.

P25 In the Book of the Watchers this watcher was called Tamiel.

P26 In the Book of the Watchers this watcher was called Chazaqiel.

P27 In the Book of the Watchers this name is missing from the list, and there are only 19 names on the list, implying one is missing, as it describes them as the "chiefs of tens" over the 200.

P28 In the Book of the Watchers this watcher was called Zaqiel. As Turel is on the list twice, Turel is likely not the original name in the text.

P29 In the Book of the Watchers this watcher was called Shamsiel, although some copies do have Simapesiel suggesting that Simapesiel may be the original in both texts.

P30 In the Book of the Watchers this watcher was called Sathariel.

P31 In the Book of the Watchers this watcher was called Yomiel, however the names Yomiel and Turiel were in the reverse order.

P32 In the Book of the Watchers this watcher was called Sariel.

P33 Azazel is on the list twice for some reason, giving a total of 21 watchers. In Book of the Watchers, there were only 19 watchers listed (Busaseial was missing), and Azazel was only listed once.

Azazel was alto mentioned the Torah, where in the book of Leviticus chapter 16, a sacrifice to Azazel was ordered alongside a sacrifice to Yahweh, when Aaron's son's died trying to perform sacrifices before the Ark of the Covenant.

Azazel is almost certainly a continuation of the Canaanite god (el) Aziz, the war-god, and god of the morning star. Whoever Azazel was, he seems to have been considered as powerful as Yahweh by the earliest Levites.

P34 Yeqon, also transliterated as Jeqon is believed to originate in the Aramaic term yokum (יָקוּם), which translates as 'he shall rise.'

P35 Asbeel is believed to originate in the Hebrew term 'zvl (עזבאל), which translates as 'abandon God.'

P36 Gadreel, also transliterated as Gadriel or Gaderel, is believed to originate in the Hebrew term gdr hl (גדר האל), which translates as 'wall of God.'

P37 Penemue is believed to originate in the Hebrew term fnm (פנימי), which translates as 'the inside.'

P38 Kasdaye, also transliterated as Kasdeja, is believed to originate in the Aramaic term chsd (כשׂדי), which translates as 'Chaldean,' a reference to the Semitic tribe of Chaldeans that lived in southern Iraq since the time of Abraham in Jewish history, and the fall of the Old Kingdom of Babylonia in archaeological history. An alternate theory is that the name is derived from the Aramaic term chsh d (כסה יד), which translates approximately as 'hidden hand,' or 'hidden power.'

P39 Chambers of the stars is likely a reference to the ancient Egyptian system of decans, or small-constellations, which was used from 10th Dynasty onward. These decans, or chambers, divided the sky into 36 small constellations along the equator.

P40 Lord Moloch is known from a few ancient Canaanite texts and was the national god of Ammon (modern Amman, the capital of Jordan) when the Torah's book of Levites was written. He is known from ancient Hebrew texts as v'l mlch (מלך בעל), also transliterated as Baʻal Moloch or Lord Moloch, however, there are several variations, including Molech, Mollok, Milcom, or Malcam. The Greek transliteration in the Septuagint was Molokh (Μολοχ), and the Latin translation in the Vulgate was Moloch, which is where the English transliteration originated.

Moloch is poorly understood Canaanite god, which appears to be earliest of the first Canaanite gods that Israelites were banned from worshiping, specifically prohibited by Moses in the Torah. The god seems to have quickly been abandoned and little evidence remains of him in the archaeological records. There is a reference to a god named MLK in the Ugaritic Texts from between 1450 and 1200 BC, which is believed to be Moloch, but little is known about that god. Based on the description of Moloch in the 4th Book of Enoch, Dream Visions, he appears to have been the sun according to the author. The idea that he was a solar god has been proposed by scholars for centuries, however, so far there is no archaeological evidence either supporting or contradicting this conclusion.

In the Book of Amos, the prophet Amos spoke out about Samaritans worshiping Moloch during the time of King Jeroboam II between 760 and 755 BC. At the time the Samaritans controlled a kingdom north of Judea in the territory of northern Israel, northern Palestinian West Bank, southern Israel, and southern Syria. This is the same territory that the books of Enoch are set in, and Amos specifically spoke out against the worshipers of Moloch worshiping a star or stars, suggesting that some of the books of Enoch could have been the holy books of the Samaritans Amos was criticizing, as clearly the Torah was not their holy book. If this is the case, then they would have been in use by 755 BC and may have had both a book from Noah's perspective and another from Methuselah's perspective.

The Syrians did later have a god known as Malakbel during the Greek era, however, this translates as 'Angel/Messenger of the Lord/Bel' not 'Moloch the Lord.' Malakbel could be a later development of Baʻal Moloch, which would point to a northern Canaanite origin, and not a southern origin were the Hebrews settled. The mention of MLK in the Ugaritic Texts also supports the northern origin, as Ugarit was one of the most northern cities also the coast of Canaan, laying on the northern coast of Syria today.

P41 Hebrew: v'l hchvvd (בעל הכבוד) often transliterated as Ba'al Hakavod. Translation: Lord of Glory (or Honor, Justice)

Ba'al Hakavod is a term that also shows up in the later books of Enoch, although in the *Book of the Watchers* it was 'Melek Hakavod' meaning 'King of Glory (or Honor, Justice) or possibly 'the Glorious (or Honorable, Just) Moloch,' as both melek and Moloch are spelled the same in Hebrew.

Astronomical Book Notes

A1 Aramaic: shmosh (שמש), also transliterated as Shapash, Shapsh, Shapu, or Shemesh.

Canaanite: shmsh (???), generally transliterated as Shemesh, or Shamash

Syriac: Shemsha (????), generally transliterated as Shemesh, or Shamash

The being described sounds like the Canaanite sun-god of the same name, who according to the book of Deuteronomy rode a chariot. In the Masoretic book of Kingdoms (Septuagint 4th Kingdoms), king Josiah banned the worship of the sun-god around 640 BC, meaning this text likely dates back to before that time.

A2 Aramaic: v'l (בעל), generally transliterated as Ba'al

Canaanite: B'l (???), generally transliterated as Ba'al

Amharic: bal (??)

Ba'al is the ancient sky-god, not the creator or father-god El, but his main son who was given dominion over the Earth. According to the Book of Hosea, the Samarians were still worshipping 'God' under the name of Ba'al in the 8th-century BC before they were conquered by the Assyrians. If the text is of Canaanite origin, then the Lord in the text was likely Ba'al Hadad, the 'Lord of Thunder' in the Canaanite pantheon.

A3 Hebrew: Yarikh (ירח). Definition: the moon, Yarikh (the Canaanite lunar god)

Yarikh was a Canaanite and Arabian god, also called Ya Rehuhm by the Sabean Arabs, Ya Rekuhn by the Mofarite Arabs, and Ya Rekan by the Ge'ez speaking Ethiopians. Yarikh was not described as being feminine, but masculine like the other Semitic Lunar gods.

The relationship between the Lord (Ba'al), moon, and sun described in the text is similar to the Trinity of Aramaic gods: Bel, Yarikh, and Yarhibol, who were worshiped in Palmyra before the worship of the Bel Marduk replaced them in the early-1st-millennium, implying the original text may date back to that time. However, Yarikh was not depicted as a goddess, but rather a god by the ancient Arameans, which implies the text was updated during the Persian or Greek eras, as both cultures saw the sun as masculine and the moon as feminine. The Persians viewed the moon as the goddess Mah (Avestan Manha, Old Persian Maha), and the sun as god Hvarekhshaeta, while the Greeks depicted the sun as the masculine Titan Helios, and later the god Apollo, and the moon as the feminine Titan Selene and later the goddess Artemis. The genders were most likely applied to the text during the translation to Hebrew from Canaanite (Paleo-Hebrew) sometime between 539 and 200 BC, as the Books of Enoch virtually disappeared by that time.

It is also believed by some scholars that Asherah may have been interpreted as a Lunar goddess, based on the crescent in her crown, however, the dominant view is that it was not a crescent, but horns.

A4 Hebrew: mrchvh (מרכבה), generally transliterated as Merkabah or Merkavah. Translation: chariots, flying-chariots

Traditionally scholars assumed they were a Christian-era collection of works, but since the discovery of the dead sea scrolls, it is apparent that the chariots were common in pre-Christian-era Jewish works as well. These flying chariots were central to the Revelation of Metatron, which is a work of unknown origin focused on Enoch's life after he was taken up to heaven, that appears to have been written as a sequel to the Book of Parables, implying the Book of Parables and the Revelation of Metatron circulated together at one point separate from the other books of Enoch. Other versions of these flying-objects in Jewish literature include the flying-wheels (אופן and גלגל) which the watchers flew around on.

In chapter 11, the flying chariots are described as 'circular chariots,' confirming that they are the same as the flying wheels in other sections of text.

As the term does not refer to a regular chariot, but specifically a flying-chariot, that term is used in this translation, except in chapter 11, where the term 'circular chariot' is translated directly.

The term 'flying-chariots' is also the direct translation of the word vimana found in the Hindu texts that were written around the same period, and therefore this concept was not unique to the Jewish culture.

A5 Hebrew: msvoshlch (מתושלח), generally transliterated as Methuselah.

In the Torah, and in the Book of the Watchers, Methuselah is the son of Enoch. This sentence, along with the references in chapters 10 and 11, is accepted as meaning the author of the Astronomy Book was Methuselah, who Enoch had explained the movement of the sun, stars, and winds to before the great flood. Some scholars have suggested that all four books other than the Book of Parables could have formed a text written from the perspective of Methuselah, however, most believe the Book of Watchers predated the rest.

A6 The Highest is a reference to God, or a god, found in many ancient religions in the region. According to the Torah, the ancient people of Jerusalem worshiped El Elyon, which translates as 'Highest God' when Abraham passed through the regions. The term Highest repeats though other early Jewish and Samaritan texts. In the Septuagint's Torah, the Highest was the God above Iaw (Yahweh).

A7 The Great Sea is an old reference to the Mediterranean Sea.

A8 The Erythraean Sea is an old name for the waters surrounding the Arabian Peninsula: the Arabian Sea, Red Sea, and the Persian Gulf.

A9 Orjares and Tomas are commonly used transliterations of obscure names. Like the names of the moon that follow, these terms are not obvious Hebrew, Aramaic, Syriac, or Canaanite terms. Some scholars transliterate Orjares as Aryares. It is theorized that Orjares could be a corruption of hrm vr (אור הרם) meaning 'potsherd sun,' and that Tomas is a corruption of chtm (חטם) meaning 'nose,' however, it requires the name to be 66% misspelled.

The names could be transliterations of the Egyptian terms Her-ur and Atum, which both were related to the Solar cults in Annu (Heliopolis). Atum was pronounced approximately as tmw in ancient Egyptian, and was the Egyptian solar and creation god that Moses likely worshiped. Her-ur was pronounced approximately as herwer in ancient Egyptian, was the Old Kingdom national God, today known as Horus the Elder. Both Atum and Her-ur were pre-dynastic and Old Kingdom gods associated with the sun, who continued to be worshiped at the temples in Annu throughout Egyptian history. If the names in the Astronomical Book are based on Her-ur and Atum, these are odd choices for any text written after the Old Kingdom, implying some sections of the Astronomical Book may date back to the Old Kingdom, unfortunately as the names of the moon are even more obscure, there is no way to confirm an Egyptian source for the names of the sun.

A10 Asonja, Ebla, Benase, and Erae are commonly used transliterations of obscure names. Like the names of the sun, these terms are not obvious Hebrew, Aramaic, Syriac, or Canaanite terms. Some scholars transliterate Asonja as Asenja, and Ebla as Abla.

There have been several theories proposed to explain the names. One theory is that the four names represent the four phases of the moon, however, the names cannot be matched to any known terms in Semitic languages, or ancient Egyptian.

A11 Milki-El was a Canaanite official in the Amarna Period. It is unknown if he was named after a star. The name does not appear later in Hebrew writings, and so this star list may date back to the Amarna period.

A12 Lord Moloch is known from a few ancient Canaanite texts and was the national god of Ammon (modern Amman, the capital of Jordan) when the Torah's book of Levites was written. He is known from ancient Hebrew texts as v'l mlch (מלך בעל), also transliterated as Ba'al Moloch or Lord Moloch, however, there are several variations, including Molech, Mollok, Milcom, or Malcam. The Greek transliteration in the Septuagint was Molokh (Μολοχ), and the Latin translation in the Vulgate was Moloch, which is where the English transliteration originated.

Moloch is poorly understood Canaanite god, which appears to be earliest of the first Canaanite gods that Israelites were banned from worshiping, specifically prohibited by Moses in the Torah. The god seems to have quickly been abandoned and little evidence remains of him in the archaeological records. There is a reference to a god named MLK (???) in the Ugaritic Texts from between 1450 and 1200 BC, which is believed to be Moloch, but little is known about that god. Based on the description of Moloch in the 4th Book of Enoch, Dream Visions, he appears to have been the sun according to the author. The idea that he was a solar god has been proposed by scholars for centuries, however, so far there is no archaeological evidence either supporting or contradicting this conclusion.

In the Book of Amos, the prophet Amos spoke out about Samaritans worshiping Moloch during the time of King Jeroboam II between 760 and 755 BC. At the time the Samaritans controlled a kingdom north of Judea in the territory of northern Israel, northern Palestinian West Bank, southern Israel, and southern Syria. This is the same territory that the books of Enoch are set in, and Amos specifically spoke out against the worshipers of Moloch worshiping a star or stars, suggesting that some of the books of Enoch could have been the holy books of the Samaritans Amos was criticizing, as clearly the Torah was not their holy book. If this is the case, then they would have been in use by 755 BC and may have had both a book from Noah's perspective and another from Methuselah's perspective.

The Syrians did later have a god known as Malakbel during the Greek era, however, this translates as 'Angel/Messenger of the Lord/Bel' not 'Moloch the Lord.' Malakbel could be a later development of Ba'al Moloch, which would point to a northern Canaanite origin, and not a southern origin were the Hebrews settled. The mention of MLK in the Ugaritic Texts also supports the northern origin, as Ugarit was one of the most northern cities also the coast of Canaan, laying on the northern coast of Syria today.

A13 Hebrew: v'l hchvvd (בעל הכבוד) often transliterated as Ba'al Hakavod. Translation: Lord of Glory (or Honor, Justice)

Ba'al Hakavod is a term that also shows up in the later books of Enoch, although in the *Book of the Watchers* it was 'Melek Hakavod' meaning 'King of Glory (or Honor, Justice) or possibly 'the Glorious (or Honorable, Just) Moloch,' as both melek and Moloch are spelled the same in Hebrew.

Dream Visions Notes

D1 Aramaic: v'l (בעל). Generally transliterated as Baal or Ba'al. Translation: owner, lord, master, or husband.

Ge'ez: bal (??)

Ba'al was the Canaanite and later Hebrew and Aramaic term which translates as 'the Lord.' If the text is of Canaanite origin, then the Lord in the text was likely Ba'al Hadad, the 'Lord of Thunder' in the Canaanite pantheon.

D2 Hebrew: tehom (תהום). Translations: deep, depths, deep sea, subterranean waters, grave

Greek: abyssos (ἀβύσσου). Translation: abyss, another name for Tartarus - the Greek primordial underworld god

The abyss is a common element in most ancient mid-east religions. It was imagined as an infinitely deep dark place, generally filled with fresh water. The Akkadians and Babylonians called in tamtu, and in Ugaritic Canaanite it was t-h-m. Both terms and the later Hebrew tehom are believed to derive from the Sumerian name Tiamat, who was a goddess that lived in the depths of the ocean. The Sumerian term for the abyss was Abzu, which is likely where the Greek term abyssos ultimately derives from. In Egyptian beliefs, the abyss was called Nu, and like many of the other religion this sea was seen as being both below the Earth, and above Sky, and reaching off to infinity. All of these concepts seem to be an early attempt to envision what is now called outer space.

D3 Lord Moloch is known from a few ancient Canaanite texts and was the national god of Ammon (modern Amman, the capital of Jordan) when the Torah's book of Levites was written. He is known from ancient Hebrew texts as v'l mlch (מלך בעל), also transliterated as Ba'al Moloch or Lord Moloch, however, there are several variations, including Molech, Mollok, Milcom, or Malcam. The Greek transliteration in the Septuagint was Molokh (Μολοχ), and the Latin translation in the Vulgate was Moloch, which is where the English transliteration originated.

Moloch is poorly understood Canaanite god, which appears to be earliest of the first Canaanite gods that Israelites were banned from worshiping, specifically prohibited by Moses in the Torah. The god seems to have quickly been abandoned and little evidence remains of him in the archaeological records. There is a reference to a god named MLK (???) in the Ugaritic Texts from between 1450 and 1200 BC, which is believed to be Moloch, but little is known about that god. Based on the description of Moloch in the 4th Book of Enoch, Dream Visions, he appears to have been the sun according to the author. The idea that he was a solar god has been proposed by scholars for centuries, however, so far there is no archaeological evidence either supporting or contradicting this conclusion.

In the Book of Amos, the prophet Amos spoke out about Samaritans worshiping Moloch during the time of King Jeroboam II between 760 and 755 BC. At the time the Samaritans controlled a kingdom north of Judea in the territory of northern Israel, northern Palestinian West Bank, southern Israel, and southern Syria. This is the same territory that the books of Enoch are set in, and Amos specifically spoke out against the worshipers of Moloch worshiping a star or stars, suggesting that some of the books of Enoch could have been the holy books of the Samaritans Amos was criticizing, as clearly the Torah was not their holy book. If this is the case, then they would have been in use by 755 BC and may have had both a book from Noah's perspective and another from Methuselah's perspective.

The Syrians did later have a god known as Malakbel during the Greek era, however, this translates as 'Angel/Messenger of the Lord/Bel' not 'Moloch the Lord.' Malakbel could be a later development of Ba'al Moloch, which would point to a northern Canaanite origin, and not a southern origin were the Hebrews settled. The mention of MLK in the Ugaritic Texts also supports the northern origin, as Ugarit was one of the most northern cities also the coast of Canaan, laying on the northern coast of Syria today.

D4 Aramaic: iri (עִיר). Translation: watcher, guardian, sentinel

The five Semitic books of Enoch all use the term watcher instead of angel, although the watchers do share some of the names of angels in Jewish, and later Christian and Islamic texts indicating they are the same group of beings.

The watchers as believed to be based on an older Sumerian and Akkadian story of the igigi. The igigi were a group of beings in the ancient Akkadian creation and flood mythology who played a similar role to the watchers in the Enochian literature. The Aramaic term 'watchers' was iri (עִיר), which the Akkadian word igigi was composed of the Akkadian words 'igi' and 'gi' meaning 'eyes' and 'penetrate sexually.' The similar nature of 'eyes' (igi) and 'watchers' (iri) is difficult to ignore, however, the 'sexual violation' of humans is what the watchers were accused of in the books of Enoch. The Book of Parables contains several terms that appear to be direct translations of Akkadian terms from the Akkadian creation and flood stories, which supports the idea that the watchers began as a Canaanite version of the igigi.

D5 This high-tower is reminiscent of the 'high watchpost' (Hara Berezaiti) in the Zoroastrian religion, which was supposed to be high above the world as well. It could indicate a Persian influence, however, is not conclusive as there were Indo-Iranians living in the Middle East among the Mitanni and Haribu in the 2nd-millenium BC.

D6 The association of dogs and Philistines is established by the death of Saul at the hands of dogs. Additionally, Philistines valued dogs highly, and major dog cemeteries have been found near their ancient cities.

D7 The lion was the national animal of Babylonia, and specifically represented the power of the king.

D8 The eagle was the national symbol of the Achaemenid Dynasty of the Persian Empire which conquered the Babylonian Empire in 539 BC and then occupied Syria, Phoenicia (Lebanon), Cyprus and Judea in 525 BC, and Egypt in 524 BC.

D9 Hebrew: v'l hchvvd (בעל הכבוד) often transliterated as Ba'al Hakavod. Translation: Lord of Glory (or Honor, Justice)

Ba'al Hakavod is a term that also shows up in the later books of Enoch, although in the *Book of the Watchers* it was 'Melek Hakavod' meaning 'King of Glory (or Honor, Justice) or possibly 'the Glorious (or Honorable, Just) Moloch,' as both melek and Moloch are spelled the same in Hebrew.

Letter of Enoch Notes

L1 The term 'Word' in this context is drawn from the Greek philosophical concept of the Logos (λόγος) which was itself developed from the common Greek expression 'lego' (λέγω) meaning 'I say.' The concept entered into Jewish though sometime during the Greek era and then entered into Gnosticism in the 1st century AD, and Christianity in the 2nd-century AD.

The term is first known to have been used by the Greek philosopher Heraclitus around 500 BC, who used the term to define a type of absolute knowledge. It was subsequently built on by Plato, Aristotle, the Sophists, Pyrrhonists, and Stoics by 300 BC.

It is unclear when the concept entered into Judaism, however, it is clear it had entered Judaism before Gnosticism or Christianity. The Jewish philosopher Philo of Alexandria used the term Logos similar to the later Gnostic and Christian circa 40 AD, when he referred to the Logos of God as being the 'Angel of the Lord' from the Septuagint, and described the Word as the 'first-born of God.' This is very similar to the Christian interpretation of the Word found in the Gospel of John, except that Jesus is identified as being the Word in the Christian version.

The fact that the Word is mentioned does cause some confusion as it stopped being used in Judaism after the Second Jewish-Roman War, and most assume it is a Christian reference. If it is the Christian term being used, it would have to be a later addition to the text, as fragments of the text have been found among the Dead Sea Scrolls dating to sometime between 300 and 200 BC, however, there is no reason to assume it is the Christian term, as the Jews had a similar term. Unfortunately, the verse in question has not been recovered among the dead sea scrolls, and therefore there is no way of knowing if the term was in the original text or added by a Christian later on. If it was in the original text, it would date the text firmly to sometime after the Greeks had taken control of Judea, and before the Maccabean Revolt, between 330 and 167 BC.

L2 The term 'Righteous' in the Ge'ez is believed to have been a translation via Greek of the Hebrew term tzdk (צדק), which is generally translated as righteous. The Hebrew word 'tzdk' formed part of the name of two Canaanite kings in the Torah and the book of Joshua: Melchizedek and Adonizedek, proving it was a Canaanite term before the Hebrews settled in Canaan. It also was the name of the High Priest Zadok from in the time of Kings David and Solomon, from whom the Zadokite priesthood took their name. The Zadokites were the major alternative priesthood to the Levites from the time that David captured Jerusalem until the Maccabean Revolt. As Zadok was not mentioned until after David conquered Jerusalem from the Jebusites, it is believed by some scholars that he was a Jebusite priest who David allowed to maintain his position after capturing the city. In this interpretation, the linage provided in the text that makes him a descendant of Aaron is considered to be a later insertion to legitimize his position. Zadok was instrumental in placing Solomon on the throne of Israel over his older brother Adonijah, which ultimately gave Zadok a lot of influence over the young king Solomon.

In Canaanite, the names Zadok, Melchizedek, and Adonizedek, do not include the word 'tzdk' meaning righteousness, but the name of the god Sydyk. Little is known about Sydyk, although his name shows up occasionally in Canaanite ruins. The Ugaritic texts from around 1300 BC mention a god named Ṣaduq who is believed to be Sydyk. The modern spelling of Sydyk is from the Greek Sydyc (Συδυκ), mentioned in Eusebius' Praeparatio Evangelica when he quoted Philo of Byblos' quote of Sanchuniathon, who was, apparently, a Canaanite author that lived in Egypt during the New Kingdom era, before 1200 BC. The accuracy of Philo's writings about Sanchuniathon is questioned as he switched fluidly between his own ideas and quotes of Sanchuniathon, nevertheless, he claimed that Elus (El) and Aphrodite (Astarte) had children called the Titanides (now accepted as a reference to the Kotharat) who married Sydyk. Based on archaeological evidence, the Kotharat appears to have been a group of midwives, and if they were married to a god, it implies they were more likely a priesthood of nuns or priestesses. The references to the 'children of righteousness' found throughout 5th Enoch sounds almost identical to the term 'sons of Zadok' from Psalms, which is generally translated as Zadokite. If the Zadokites were a continuation of a Canaanite priesthood, then they may have been the vehicle through which the books of Job and Enoch literature passed into the Israelite religion.

The righteousness described in this Letter a 'light,' opposed to 'darkness' and 'lies,' mirroring of the Zoroastrian conflict between the 'light' asha, meaning 'righteousness' or 'truth,' and 'dark' druj, meaning 'lies' or 'falsehood.' While the concept of 'following the law' is certainly consistently with Judaism at the time (or any time), much of the text of the Letter is unique so Judaism, and appear to be heavily influenced by Zoroastrianism, while remaining essentially Jewish.

L3 Holy Lord is a unique term to the 5th Book of Enoch, and not found in the first four, indicating a separate author at a later date. The term Holy Lord is also not found in the Masoretic Texts or the Septuagint. A similar phrase 'Lord of Saints' (κυρίου τοῦ ἁγίου) in the Christianized Septuagint is sometimes translated 'Holy Lord,' however, is a 3rd-century Christian redaction of the 'god Iaw' (θεός ΙΑΩ), Iaw being the ancient transliteration of Yhwh, commonly translated as Yahweh or Jehovah today. The Masoretic Texts have 'kdvosh yhwh lhm' (קדוש יהוה אלהים) meaning 'sacred god Iaw,' which means the author of the Letter of Enoch could not have been referencing this term found in Masoretic Samuel and the Septuagint's 1st Kingdoms. It is possible that the Letter once contained 'holy Iaw' (קדוש יהוה), however, there is no other evidence of Iaw in the various books of Enoch, until the Revelation of Metatron.

L4 Wisdom is also a goddess or spirit of some kind in the Hebrew book of Proverbs, which is traditionally attributed to Solomon, however, is now known to be a compilation of Proverbs, some of which were copied from the much older Wisdom of Amenenope. In the Hebrew texts, the word chchmvs (חכמות) is used, which is often described as a 'feminine plural indefinite form' of chchm (חכם), meaning 'sage,' 'wisdom,' or 'clever.' The Greeks at the Library of Alexandria translated the Hebrew term chchmvs (חכמות) as Sophia (Σοφία) meaning wisdom and treated her as a type of spirit or god within the text. She was later adopted by the Gnostics of the 2nd-century AD, where she was sometimes described as the wife of God, or the wife of Jesus, or an Aeon which was a type of lesser god.

The nature of the Hebrew term has been debated for thousands of years and could have stated as a reference to the Priestess of Chmvsh (כמוש), more commonly known as the Moabite god as Chemosh. He is recorded in several ancient Canaanite and Israelite documents including the Mesha Stele from circa 840 BC, various Elbite tablets from between 3500 and 700 BC. According to the 3rd Kingdoms chapter 11, King Solomon built a Temple to Chemosh on the Mount of Olives, which according to 4th Kingdoms chapter 23, was later torn down by King Josiah when he instituted his 'one god policy.' As the term used here denotes a sentient being, the Greek Sophia is used in the translation, although 'Priestess of Chemosh' might be more appropriate if translating from the Hebrew.

The use of Sophia (Σοφία) as a translation for chchmvs (חכמות) was already present in the Septuagint's book of Proverbs by 132 BC, and therefore was not something that originated with the Christians or Gnostics. In Proverbs, she was depicted similarly to the way she is depicted in the Book of Parables. It is likely that this section of the book dates to the Greek era, between 330 and 150 BC, however, could also have originated in the Persian era under the influence of the Persian goddess Anahita, who was also a wisdom-goddess, or much earlier in the Canaanite era under the influence of the Egyptian goddess Seshat, the goddess of wisdom, knowledge, and writing.

L5 The weeks in the Letter of Enoch are often assumed to be related to the calendar in the Book of Jubilees, however, there is no way to correlate the weeks of Enoch with that calendar. The weeks in the Jubilees calendar were seven years long, and Enoch was not born when Adam was seven years old. The Book of Jubilees was endorsed as an official text by the Hasmonean Dynasty around 140 BC as it included a prediction of the Maccabean Revolt, which resulted in the Hasmoneans ruling an independent Judea. Based on the prediction of the Maccabean Revolt, the Book of Jubilees is generally assumed to date to the beginning of the Maccabean Revolt, sometime between 167 and 160 BC. The fact that the Book of Jubilees included the name of Noah's wife and other details found in the 4th Book of Enoch, Dream Visions, it is now accepted that the Book of Jubilees drew from the Enochian literature, and therefore the idea of the 'weeks' could have been adopted from the Letter of Enoch.

The actual time-span described as a 'week' in the Letter of Enoch appears dependent on the prediction in the much older Book of the Watchers, in which Enoch predicted the end of the world would come 10,000 years after his time. It's unclear which chronology the author would have used, as, in the Masoretic text Enoch lived between 622 and 987 AM (MT), while in the Greek Septuagint Enoch lived between 1122 and 1487 AM (GS), and in the Samaritan Torah Enoch lived between 522 and 887 AM (ST). As a result of the differences in the texts, there are different versions of the Anno Mundi calendar, which based on the number of years since Adam was created in the various Israelite religions. Given the differences in the texts, the Enochian prediction of the end of the world can only be placed into the broad time-span of sometime between 10,500 and 11,500 AM. By the Persian era, this time-span would have looked like the Zoroastrian 12,000-year cycle. Given the descriptions of the end-of-the-world in the Book of Parables, chapter 22, repeated in this book in chapter 1, it is clear there was a Zoroastrian influence in these texts. If the ten 'weeks' are 1200 years long each, then the length of the 10 'weeks' would have been 12,000 years, and Enoch would have been born in the first 'week' regardless of the texts used.

Conversely, the calendar described in the book of Jubilees treats 49 year periods as 'Jubilees,' which, if one were to group into a 'week' of 7 jubilees would still only add up to 343 years. All versions of the Hebrew scriptures place the birth of Enoch significantly later than 343 AM. Carrying the idea of jubilee weeks forward, the world would have ended in 3430 AM, which would have been circa 344 BC (MT), or 2104 BC (GS), or 985 BC (ST). Yet, this Letter has clear Greek influence, indicating it was written sometime after 330 BC. It seems unlikely the author would have been predicting that the world had already ended, and therefore something other than the Jubilee calendar has to be used. Additionally, at no point in the Book of Jubilees are jubilees grouped this way, only groups of seven years are called 'weeks.'

BOOKS OF ENOCH COLLECTION 219

Grouping together very long spans of years was not uncommon at the time and was connected to flood mythology long before the Enochian literature was written. Sumerians had used spans of 600 years, called 'ners,' and even longer periods of 3600 years called 'sars,' which were still used in later periods for measuring the length of time before the flood of Ziusudra.

Assuming the 1200 year long 'week,' the eighth 'week' is approximately 4626 to 5825 AD (Masoretic Texts), or 2866 to 4065 AD (Septuagint), or 3985 to 5184 AD (Samaritan Torah).

L6 Hebrew: mlk hchvvd (מלך הכבוד) often transliterated as Melek Hakavod or Hakavod Moloch. Translation: Lord of Glory / Honor / Justice or Glorious / Honorable / Just Moloch

Ba'al Hakavod is a term that also shows up in the earlier books of Enoch, although sometimes shows up as 'Melek Hakavod' here meaning 'King of Glory / Honor / Justice' or possibly 'the Glorious / Honorable / Just Moloch,' as both melek and Moloch are spelled the same in Hebrew. It is unlikely that the author of the Letter of Enoch meant 'Moloch' at this later period, and most likely was simply copying the term from older books of Enoch.

L7 Assuming the 1200 year-long 'week,' the ninth 'week' is approximately 5826 to 7025 AD (Masoretic Texts), or 4066 to 5265 AD (Septuagint), or 5185 to 6384 AD (Samaritan Torah).

L8 Assuming the 1200 year-long 'week,' the tenth 'week' is approximately 7026 to 8225 AD (Masoretic Texts), or 5266 to 6465 AD (Septuagint), or 6385 to 7584 AD (Samaritan Torah).

This same description of the end-of-the-world is found in Book of Parables, implying Parables was being used by the Enochians by the time the Letter of Enoch was written. This description is identical to the anachronistic description of the end-of-the-world found in the Book of Parables. Most of the Book of Parables points to a Babylonian origin, however, this Zoroastrian end-of-the-world description cannot predate the Persian era within an Israelite text.

The final destruction of darkness by Ahura Mazda (Lord of Wisdom), is a central theme of the Zoroastrian end of the world, which this verse seems to be paraphrasing. The author of this Letter may have been the person that inserted this line, and possibly the person who unified the four older books with this letter.

L9 Enoch was in the seventh generation from Adam in the Torah.

L10 Assuming the 1200 year-long 'week,' the first 'week' is approximately 3774 to 2575 BC (Masoretic Texts), or 5534 to 4335 BC (Septuagint), or 4415 to 3216 BC (Samaritan Torah). For reference, Enoch's life was approximately between 3152 and 2787 BC (Masoretic Texts), or 4412 and 4047 BC (Septuagint), or 3893 and 3528 BC (Samaritan Torah).

L11 Assuming the 1200 year-long 'week,' the second 'week' is approximately 2574 to 1375 BC (Masoretic Texts), or 4334 to 3135 BC (Septuagint), or 3215 to 2016 BC (Samaritan Torah).

L12 Assuming the 1200 year-long 'week,' Noah's flood was approximately 2118 BC (Masoretic Texts), or 3298 BC (Septuagint), or 3108 BC (Samaritan Torah).

L13 Assuming the 1200 year-long 'week,' the third 'week' is approximately 1374 to 175 BC (Masoretic Texts), or 3134 to 1935 BC (Septuagint), or 2015 to 816 BC (Samaritan Torah).

Determining who this person is, is difficult because of the three different chronologies in the texts. If the author used Masorite-like texts, this could be considered a prediction of the Maccabean Revolt which started in 167 BC, eight years after 175 BC.

If the author used Septuagint-like texts then the date given corresponds to the time that Isaac and Jacob were alive, and Jacob's sons, the 12 Patriarchs, were born starting with Reuben was born circa 1941 BC, followed by Simeon in 1940 BC, and Levi in 1939 BC, Dan in 1938 BC, Naphtali in 1937 BC, Gad in 1936 BC, Asher in 1934 BC, Issachar in 1929 BC, Zebulun in 1927 BC, Judah in 1922 BC, Joseph in 1917 BC. Given that the Levites were the religious cast of Samaria and Judea, it seems likely their patriarch Levi is the son of Jacob referred to here.

The Samaritan Chronicle doesn't indicate anything significant within a decade of 816 BC, however, although it was approximately the era of Jehoash of King of Judah, who ordered the repair of Solomon's Temple according to the Masoretic Texts. As the Samaritans do not believe in Solomon's Temple, it is unlikely that the author was a Samaritan referring to this event.

This is often assumed to be a reference to the Maccabean Revolt, even though there is no evidence of the Hasmoneans endorsing the Letter of Enoch as they did with the Book of Jubilees which did include a prediction of the Revolt that they accepted, and therefore the reference to the era the 12 Patriarchs were born seems more likely.

L14 Assuming the 1200-year-long 'week,' the fourth 'week' is approximately 174 BC to 1025 AD (Masoretic Texts), or 1934 to 735 BC (Septuagint), or 815 BC to 384 AD (Samaritan).

The Septuagint chronology here refers to the lifetime of Isaiah, the prophet that spawned the Messianic movement within Judaism.

L15 Assuming the 1200-year-long 'week,' the fifth 'week' is approximately 1026 to 2225 AD (Masoretic Texts), or 734 BC to 465 AD (Septuagint), or 385 BC to 1584 AD (Samaritan).

L16 Assuming the 1200-year-long 'week,' the sixth 'week' is approximately 2226 to 3425 AD (Masoretic Texts), or 466 to 1665 AD (Septuagint), or 1585 to 2784 AD (Samaritan).

L17 Assuming the 1200-year-long 'week,' the seventh 'week' is approximately 3426 to 4625 AD (Masoretic Texts), or 1666 to 2865 AD (Septuagint), or 2785 to 3984 AD (Samaritan).

L18 Ge'ez: Sayireni (????)

Greek: Siren (Σειρήν)

The word 'siren' is found in the Septuagint in places where the Masoretic Texts have 'lilis' (לִילִית) which translates as 'owls.' There is no evidence for the Jews or Samaritans having Sirens in their belief system before the Greek era, however, it seems improbable the translators at the Library of Alexandria would have mistranslated 'owl' as 'siren.' Siren began in Greek mythology as half-bird people, however, depictions of them changed into mermaids by the Middle Ages. Ancient Greek statues of Sirens depict them as women with wings like angels but the feet of birds like the Roman Harpies, and virtually identical to the Burney Relief from ancient Babylon, circa 1800 BC. The question of what exactly the Burney Relief depicts had been debated for most of the past century, with varying opinions including the Sumerian goddess Inanna, the Akkadian goddess Eresh-Kigal, or perhaps a Babylonian lilitu, which was a type of night-demon. The Babylonian lilitu was a poorly understood demon, who seems to have played the same role as the Roman Succubus. The word 'lilis' in the Masoretic Texts book of Isaiah, appears as 'liliyyot' in the Great Isaiah Scroll (1Q1Isa) found among the Dead Sea Scrolls. The word 'liliyyot' is generally translated as 'Lilith,' the name of a Hebrew demon, similar to the lilitu from Babylonian mythology. Given that the translators of the Septuagint chose to translate the word in the text they had of Isaiah as 'siren' it is plausible that they had a copy of Isaiah with the term 'liliyyot' in it instead of Lilith, which would imply that this was the same term originally used in the Letter of Enoch. The term Lilith is unknown in Hebrew or Canaanite literature before the Babylonian era and is believed to have been adopted by some of the Jews in Babylon from ancient Babylonian demonology. The demons were known within Mesopotamian religions from the Sumerian era onward.

L19 This is a reference to Tyrian Purple dye, one of Phoenicia's most expensive exports. In the 4th-century BC, the Greek historian Theopompus noted, 'Purple for dyes fetched its weight in silver at Colophon.' Colophon was an ancient town near modern Değirmendere Fev in western Turkey.

L20 Hebrew: nefesh (נֶפֶשׁ). Translation: mind, life, soul, person

Greek: psychên (ψυχήν). Translation: mind, personality, psyche

This is generally used only in relation to humans and angels who have a more developed mind.

Available Digitally

SEPTUAGINT SERIES:

1. Septuagint: Genesis
2. Septuagint: Exodus
3. Septuagint: Leviticus
4. Septuagint: Numbers
5. Septuagint: Deuteronomy
6. Septuagint: Joshua
7. Septuagint: Judges
8. Septuagint: Ruth
9. Septuagint: 1st Kingdoms
10. Septuagint: 2nd Kingdoms
11. Septuagint: 3rd Kingdoms
12. Septuagint: 4th Kingdoms
13. Septuagint: 1st Paraleipomenon
14. Septuagint: 2nd Paraleipomenon
15. Septuagint: 1st Ezra
16. Septuagint: 2nd Ezra
17. Septuagint: Tobit
18. Septuagint: Judith
19. Septuagint: Esther
20. Septuagint: 1st Maccabees
21. Septuagint: 2nd Maccabees
22. Septuagint: 3rd Maccabees
23. Septuagint: 4th Maccabees
24. Septuagint: Psalms
25. Septuagint: Prayer of Manasses
26. Septuagint: Job
27. Septuagint: Proverbs
28. Septuagint: Ecclesiastes

29. Septuagint: Song of Songs

SEPTUAGINT COLLECTIONS:

Septuagint: Torah

Septuagint: Orit

Septuagint: Histories

Septuagint: The Kingdoms Collection

Septuagint: The Paraleipomenons Collection

Septuagint: The Ezras Collection

Septuagint: The Maccabees Collection

THE LIFE OF ADAM AND EVE:

1. Apocalypse of Moses
2. Latin Life of Adam and Eve
3. Penitence of Adam
4. Slavonic Life of Adam and Eve
5. Book of Adam

BOOKS OF ENOCH AND METATRON:

1. Book of the Watchers
2. Book of Parables
3. Astronomical Book
4. Dream Visions
5. Letter of Enoch
6. Secrets of Enoch
7. Ascension of Moses
8. Revelation of Metatron

BOOKS OF ENOCH COLLECTION

TESTAMENTS OF THE PATRIARCHS:

1. Testament of Adam
2. 1st Testament of Abraham
3. 2nd Testament of Abraham
4. Testament of Isaac
5. Testament of Jacob
6. Testament of Reuben
7. Testament of Simeon
8. Testament of Levi
9. Testament of Judah
10. Testament of Issachar
11. Testament of Zebulun
12. Testament of Dan
13. Testament of Naphtali
14. Testament of Gad
15. Testament of Asher
16. Testament of Joseph
17. Testament of Benjamin
18. Testament of Job
19. Testament of Moses
20. Testament of Solomon

TESTAMENTS OF THE PATRIARCHS COLLECTIONS:

The Testaments of Abraham Collection

The Testaments of Abraham, Isaac, and Jacob Collection

Testaments of the Twelve Patriarchs Collection

Testaments of the Patriarchs Collection

APOCALYPSE OF EZRA:

1. Jewish Apocalypse of Ezra
2. Latin Apocalypse of Ezra
3. Greek Apocalypse of Ezra

OTHER TEXTS:

Letter of Aristeas and the Pithom Stele

Three Steles of Seth

Wisdom of Amenemope

Words of Ahikar

OTHER COLLECTIONS:

Apocalypses of Ezra Collection

Books of Enoch Collection

Books of Enoch and Metatron Collection

Books of Metatron Collection

Life of Adam and Eve Collection

Septuagint's Job and the Testament of Job

Septuagint's Proverbs and the Wisdom of Amenemope

Available in Print

SEPTUAGINT SERIES:

Septuagint: Torah

Septuagint: Orit

Septuagint: Histories (Volume 1)

Septuagint: Histories (Volume 2)

Septuagint: The Kingdoms Collection

Septuagint: The Paraleipomenons Collection

Septuagint: The Ezras Collection

Septuagint: The Maccabees Collection

ENOCH AND METATRON SERIES:

Books of Enoch Collection

Books of Enoch and Metatron Collection

Books of Metatron Collection

Secrets of Enoch

OTHER COLLECTIONS:

Septuagint's Job and the Testament of Job

Septuagint's Proverbs and the Wisdom of Amenemope

Testaments of the Patriarchs Collection

Milton Keynes UK
Ingram Content Group UK Ltd.
UKHW041304241023
431246UK00004B/549